ROBINSON-PATMAN ACT

POSNER, R.

U·M·I Books on Demand™

This

U·M·I
BOOKS ON DEMAND

University Microfilms International
A Bell & Howell Company

300 North Zeeb Road
P.O. Box 1346
Ann Arbor, Michigan 48106-1346
1-800-521-0600   313-761-4700

Printed in 1995 by xerographic process
on acid-free paper

The
Robinson-Patman Act

Federal Regulation of Price Differences

Richard A. Posner

American Enterprise Institute for Public Policy Research
Washington, D. C.

Richard A. Posner is professor of law at the University of Chicago Law School.

ISBN 0-8447-3228-1

Library of Congress Catalog Card No. 76-47964

(Government Regulation 1) (AEI Studies 131)

Printed in the United States of America

CONTENTS

FOREWORD

Understanding how the Robinson-Patman Act—an anticompetition measure that directly contradicts the spirit of our antitrust laws—found a place among our statutes is difficult unless we know the conditions and emotions of the 1930s—especially the desperation abroad in the United States. Although many complain today of the downward rigidity of prices and their upward flexibility (sometimes called the ratchet effect [1]), the great problem of the 1930s was thought to be a downward flexibility that led to a self-sustaining downward spiral once price cuts started. The National Industry Recovery Act (NIRA) and the Agricultural Adjustment Act were passed to stop the price slide and to introduce downward rigidity. NIRA suspended the antitrust laws and urged firms to enter cartels—this because the horrendous deflation of 1929–1933 was mistakenly attributed to the forces of competition. Under this law a neighborhood pants presser was sent to jail for pressing a suit for a nickel less than the price mandated under a National Recovery Administration (NRA) code.[2]

The Supreme Court ruled NIRA unconstitutional on May 27, 1935. Immediately following the decision, on June 11, the Robinson-Patman Act was introduced in Congress to restore many of the provisions of the defunct law, especially those designed to produce downward price rigidity. Much of the con-

---

[1] Stephen Lustgarten, *Industrial Concentration and Inflation* (Washington, D.C.: American Enterprise Institute, 1975), pp. 18-20.

[2] Jacob Maged of Paterson, New Jersey, served three days for pressing a suit for 35 cents rather than 40 cents. See *New York Times*, April 21, 1934, p. 8, col. 8, and April 24, 1934, p. 25, col. 4.

gressional debate gave vent to the anti-chain-store emotion abroad in the land. Because chain stores had a reputation for price cutting, measures to outlaw them were suggested. (Several states passed laws taxing chain stores with rates per store increasing steeply with the number in a chain.) Instead, Robinson-Patman was passed.

It was said that the act would maintain independent, individually owned stores. Ironically, the law has been used to prevent associations of independent merchants from obtaining the same discounts from manufacturers that wholesalers and jobbers obtain, as Professor Posner says in this study. One of the FTC's bureaus has pointed out that this action is leading to the replacement of small businesses by chains—a result of the act which was supposed to be prevented by it—and to protection of the profits of large firms at the expense of small firms (and consumers).

> The Commission's past Robinson-Patman efforts were directed in part to preventing cooperative groups (contract chains, in effect) of warehouse distributors from obtaining price reductions from parts manufacturers. To the extent that past Commission action has been successful in preventing contract chains from getting these lower prices and to the extent that they continue to be available, it is not surprising to find ownership chains arising in an attempt to obtain them. Thus, in a very real sense it can be said that past Commission action (enforcement of Robinson-Patman) has contributed to the merger trend now observed.
>
> If this analysis is correct, present attempts to prevent horizontal ownership integration (merger) from taking place may be assimilated to the previous attack on the contract integrations that were created to obtain (and apparently did obtain) lower prices from parts manufacturers. The present merger enforcement program will have the same effect, if successful, as past enforcement of the Robinson-Patman Act had. It will protect the high margins of parts manufacturers.[3]

Despite Robinson-Patman's avowed aim of supporting the continued existence of a distribution network of independent merchants, it has made it difficult for manufacturers to give to "mom and pop" stores the aid they would like to give to make

---

[3] Federal Trade Commission, Office of Policy Planning and Evaluation, *1976 Budget Overview*, ATRR, No. 692 (December 10, 1974), p. E-10.

sure these small businesses survive. If a local discount house buys a manufacturer's obsolescent or special low-cost model of an appliance and offers a bargain, a company like RCA cannot, under the Robinson-Patman Act, offer its competing model at a reduced price to the locally competing independent appliance stores in order to maintain their viability unless it reduces its price nationally.[4] To do so makes the price cut for local purposes a much too expensive means of preserving these independent merchants as a part of RCA's distribution network. In such cases, the result of Robinson-Patman pricing restrictions has, therefore, been to hurt rather than help small operators. The act has tended to prevent the downward flexibility in prices that is so much desired in this era of inflation (and especially in periods of "stagflation"). It prevents sporadic price discrimination, and this sporadic price discrimination is the beginning of systematically lower prices throughout an industry, as Professor Posner shows.

According to the Supreme Court in its notorious *Utah Pie* decision, the "evil" of sporadic price discrimination lies in its "contribut[ion] to what proved to be a deteriorating price structure."[5] Without sporadic price discrimination, prices tend to move from a higher price level toward a new equilibrium much more slowly than they would otherwise. The "long run" becomes much longer.

The overwhelming number of absurdities resulting from the application of the Robinson-Patman Act by the Federal Trade Commission (FTC) and the courts makes it difficult to pick any one to illustrate undesirable features of the act. However, in this day of concern with economy in the use of energy, one does stand out. The Federal Energy Administration (FEA) has estimated that one of the FTC's rulings under Robinson-Patman wastes up to 100 million gallons of truck fuel annually and costs the nation $300 million in resources devoted to unneeded transportation.[6]

The ruling in question made it uneconomic for buyers to fill their trucks on otherwise empty backhauls with the goods to be delivered to them by suppliers' trucks. It was illegal for customers picking up their own goods with their own trucks at

[4] Testimony of a witness from RCA before the Domestic Council Review Group cited in "Draft DCRG Robinson-Patman Report" (unpublished, March 8, 1976), p. 125.

[5] Utah Pie Co. v. Continental Baking Co. et al., 386 U.S. 690 (1967).

[6] Letter from Frank Zarb, dated August 15, 1975, to Lewis Engman, chairman, Federal Trade Commission.

supplier distribution facilities to receive a lower price from manufacturers who sell at delivered prices. In some trades, suppliers could not legally offer customers f.o.b. dock prices or delivery cost rebates from delivered prices. Since buyers could not be given any saving on delivered prices—that would be a rebate and "unfair" to those not having trucks with empty backhauls—their trucks did not find it worthwhile to take the extra time to fill an otherwise empty backhaul. As a consequence, suppliers unnecessarily burned millions of gallons of gasoline and diesel fuel delivering goods that could have been hauled by buyers' trucks passing suppliers' warehouses empty on the way back from deliveries.

Under pressure from the National Commission on Productivity the FTC amended its Robinson-Patman rule to allow manufacturers to offer *both* f.o.b. prices and delivered prices. But the f.o.b. prices must be uniform to all customers despite the fact that the supplier's cost of delivery to distant customers is greater than his cost to nearby customers. A uniform delivered price, as Professor Posner points out, discriminates in favor of distant customers. This is not labeled discrimination under Robinson-Patman, however, since the act holds that price differences among customers are discriminatory and uniform prices nondiscriminatory. The result is that it still does not pay many of a manufacturer's distant customers to take advantage of f.o.b. prices even when social economies would result.

The use of a uniform f.o.b. price represents some improvement over the situation where there is only a uniform delivered price. Efficiency is encouraged by giving a lower price to at least some nearby customers, as well as to customers whose trucks pass very close to suppliers, than to distant customers more costly to serve. As Professor Posner shows, this encourages cost-saving location decisions. Nevertheless, large wastes remain because backhaul allowances cannot be proportioned to the delivery costs saved by suppliers when customers pick up their own goods. To illustrate, a Kansas City wholesaler is supplied by a St. Louis manufacturer who provides a uniform backhaul allowance of twenty-four cents per hundredweight (the cost of delivery in St. Louis). The wholesaler's trucks make deliveries to points only sixty miles from St. Louis. It does not pay the wholesaler to send his trucks on to St. Louis to pick up his goods for the twenty-four-cent saving. His trucks, therefore, return empty to Kansas City while the manufacturer delivers goods to him in other trucks at a cost to the manufacturer of ninety-nine cents per hundredweight. While this evil arises from the discrimination inherent in the uniform delivered price system, the presumably antidiscriminatory Robinson-Patman restrictions prevent the manufacturer from arranging his pricing to provide sufficient variety to different customers to mitigate this evil and still remain competitive in areas he wishes to serve. A proportional backhaul allowance would do no more, at most, than maintain the current discrimination inherent in uniform delivered prices.[7] It would have the advantage, however, of eliminating some of the wastes inherent in a uniform delivered price system.

Professor Posner opposes the Robinson-Patman Act for many reasons. They range from (1) the fact that "many cost-justified price differences have . . . been suppressed" through (2) the act's serious interference "with the efficient functioning of the economy" and (3) its deleterious effects on small business outweighing the protection it has given them to (4) the fact that the FTC is forcing firms to violate the Sherman Act and condoning the violations in the name of observing Robinson-Patman. He is concerned about the possibilities of predatory price discrimination, but he suggests that predatory pricing is adequately covered by other antitrust laws. "There is no need for a statute that supplements the Sherman Act's prohibitions against predatory pricing." Many economists have reached the conclusion that we need not even be concerned by the possibility of predatory pricing. Professor David Kamerschen tells us that

> I think there is something of a consensus among industrial organization economists that true predation is very unusual, probably illogical, and not a serious social problem in the U.S. The following quotations from respected scholars in this area should suffice to illustrate this consensus: (1) Elzinga . . . "Predatory price cutting, given its unlikely occurrence and visual similarity to healthy business rivalry, should be well down the priority list of the antitrust authorities"; (2) Dewey . . . "From the foregoing remarks, it also follows that predatory price-cutting constitutes a minor threat to competition,"; (3) Scherer . . . "Distinguishing price cutting with predatory intent from price cutting in good faith to meet tough local competi-

---

[7] Instead of the backhaul allowance being thought of as a "rebate" to a customer, it should be thought of as a payment for hauling goods where the payment is made to a customer who happens to operate trucks instead of being made to a specialized trucker.

tion is singularly difficult . . . It is fair to say that the predatory pricing doctrine is one of the shakiest pillars of existing antimerger law. Its absence would not be mourned by lovers of competition and/or logic."; and (4) Scherer . . . "In actual situations the line between meeting competition and destroying it is seldom sharp, since a great deal depends upon intent, which is hard to pin down." The legal profession seems equally outspoken as how threatening a "clog on competition" is predation, arguing that the dangers of predation are few in principle, unlikely in occurrence, and speculative in demonstration.[8]

The question is not whether predatory pricing needs to be covered under the antitrust laws, inasmuch as it is covered—by the Sherman Act. Repeal of the Robinson-Patman Act would not make predatory pricing legal. Professor Posner finds—I believe correctly—that "the repeal of the Robinson-Patman Act would not leave any gap in the control of genuinely anticompetitive practices."

Graduate School of Business   Yale Brozen
University of Chicago

---

[8] D. R. Kamerschen, "Predatory Pricing, Vertical Integration and Market Foreclosure: The Case of Ready Mix Concrete in Memphis," *Industrial Organization Review*, vol. 2, no. 2 (1974), p. 144, fn. 12, citing K. Elzinga, "Predatory Pricing: The Case of the Gunpowder Trust," *Journal of Law and Economics*, vol. 13, no. 1 (April 1970), p. 240; D. Dewey, "Competitive Policy and National Goals: The Doubtful Relevance of Antitrust," in A. Philips, ed., *Perspectives on Antitrust Policy* (Princeton, N.J.: Princeton University Press, 1965), p. 81; F. Scherer, *Industrial Market Performance and Economic Structure* (Chicago: Rand McNally, 1970), pp. 484, 202.

THE ROBINSON-PATMAN ACT

INTRODUCTION

The Robinson-Patman Act [1] is a complex statute regulating pricing and other practices in the distribution of goods. It was passed forty years ago, in 1936, ostensibly to curb price discrimination. Since its passage it has been by far the most controversial of the antitrust statutes—in fact it is almost uniformly condemned by professional and academic opinion, legal and economic. [2] Today, as part of a general interest in the deregulation of U.S. business, there is talk of repeal or substantial modification of the act. [3] Despite a paucity of hard data, this study attempts an evaluation of the Robinson-Patman Act and its enforcement.

Section I of the study discusses the economic phenomena with which the act was designed to deal. The subject of the act is "discrimination" in prices and services but we shall see that the word has a meaning in the act different from the meaning that an economist would assign to it. Of course, the fact that the act may regulate a practice that is not price discrimination in the economic sense is not necessarily a criticism of the act. For this

---

[1] 49 Stat. 1526 (1936). Section 1 of the act amended section 2 of the Clayton Act, 15 U.S.C., sec. 13. Section 3 of the act created a new criminal offense but is seldom invoked. The other sections of the act are peripheral and will not be discussed in this study.

[2] For a representative criticism, written some years ago by the current attorney general of the United States, see Edward H. Levi, "The Robinson-Patman Act—Is It in the Public Interest?" *ABA Antitrust Section*, vol. 1 (1952), p. 60ff.

[3] At this writing, the Department of Justice is in the process of formulating a proposal for a substantial overhaul of the act.

1

reason Section I both discusses the economist's concept of price discrimination (indicating how law might deal with that phenomenon) and describes other pricing practices (arguably within the scope of the act) that might call for government regulation on one ground or another—if not necessarily an economic ground.

Section II discusses the background, provisions, and course of interpretation and enforcement of the act. We shall see that the act has roots that go back many years before its passage, and that the administration of the act over a period of forty years has given it a life of its own that is probably different from what was envisaged for it by its framers.

Section III takes a closer look at the specific provisions of the act. It explains the practical meaning of the act's main provisions and attempts to evaluate the consequences (including possible economic or social justifications of those consequences) of each such provision as it has been interpreted. The conclusion in Section III is that the act serves no significant economic or social purpose—on the contrary, it is clearly opposed to the public interest.

Section IV asks what is to be done. The choice is between reform and repeal, and there I explain why my strong preference is for repeal.

I. ECONOMIC AND SOCIAL ASPECTS OF PRICE DISCRIMINATION AND PRICE DIFFERENCES

Section 1 of the Robinson-Patman Act (the act's main provision) overhauled section 2 of the Clayton Act of 1914, a section forbidding price discrimination that might substantially lessen competition.[4] Just how the Robinson-Patman Act altered the old section 2 is examined in some detail later in this study. For now, the point to grasp is that the primary thrust of section 2 of the Clayton Act, as amended by the Robinson-Patman Act, remains hostility to anticompetitive price discrimination. A further point to note, however, is that discrimination as the act defines it is simply a price difference.[5] As we shall see, this makes price discrimination as a term of legal art significantly different from price discrimination as an economic concept. However, since

---

[4] 38 Stat. 730 (1914).

[5] FTC v. Anheuser-Busch, Inc., 363 U.S. 536 (1960).

price discrimination in the economic sense often (though not always) involves price differences, the subject of the Robinson-Patman Act at least overlaps the economic phenomenon called price discrimination, and one's attitude toward the desirability of legal controls over price discrimination is bound to affect one's attitude toward the Robinson-Patman Act. There is the further possibility that the price differences forbidden by the act may conflict with other social policies, whether or not the differences are discriminatory and whether or not discrimination in the economic sense should be forbidden. Accordingly, after examining the economics of price discrimination, this section of the study will consider the possible noneconomic objections to the kinds of price differences that might be held to violate the act.

The Economics of Price Discrimination and Discriminatory Monopoly. To an economist price discrimination means making two (or more) sales at prices that are not in the same proportion to the marginal cost of each sale.[6] This rather cumbersome definition is necessary to deal with the case where charging the same price in two sales is discriminatory in the economic sense because the seller's costs differ between the two sales. For example, let us consider the case where two customers are located at different distances from the seller's plant. In this case, if the seller charges a single price to the two customers for the goods delivered at the customer's location, he is engaged in price discrimination because the cost of selling to the more distant customer is bound to be greater than the cost of selling to the closer.[7]

There are two economic objections to price discrimination. The first is that a price difference not justified by a difference in cost may distort competitive relationships and impair efficiency at the customer level. The two customers in the last example may be in competition, and the higher price relative to cost charged the nearer customer may eliminate or reduce a competitive advantage that he would otherwise have enjoyed and that would have been justified by the lower social costs of his business. This customer may have deliberately sought to econo-

---

[6] See George J. Stigler, *The Theory of Price*, 3d ed. (New York: Macmillan Co., 1966), p. 209.

[7] Were there an offsetting cost reduction involved in the sale to the distant but not to the nearer purchaser, then of course the sales would not be discriminatory.

mize on his costs of production by locating his plant near an important source of supply. If the supplier refuses to recognize the cost advantage sought by the customer's locational choice, efficiency in the customer's market may be reduced, and firms that should be encouraged (from the standpoint of economizing on overall social costs) to relocate their plants nearer their sources of supply will not be confronted by prices that provide such encouragement.

The second economic objection to price discrimination is that it is a symptom of—and, more important, a condition fostering—monopoly or cartel pricing at the seller level. If a product is being sold at the same price to two different purchasers though the costs of sale are different, or at different prices though the costs of sale are the same, this implies that the price that is higher relative to cost is yielding a profit in the economic sense.[8]

Here I must pause briefly to distinguish between "profit" in its normal accounting sense and "profit" in its technical economic sense. The former refers to the excess of revenues over the expenses of a business, with the expenses not including the cost of attracting and holding the equity capital required for the operation of the business. Were the cost of equity capital included in costs for accounting purposes, then the total revenues of a competitive firm in long-run equilibrium would be just equal to its costs, where "cost" would now include the normal return to shareholders in a corporation of the firm's risk class. Thus the normal competitive firm in equilibrium does not have profits in an economic sense. The economist reserves the term profit for an excess of revenues over total costs *including* a reasonable return on equity capital.

The economic definition of price discrimination assumes that costs are measured in their true economic sense. This means that the price that is lowest relative to cost of the different prices charged by the discriminating seller must be equal to or higher than the firm's cost of making the sale—to sell at a lower price would involve an avoidable loss—and that the higher price must exceed the firm's cost and hence include "profit" in the economic rather than accounting sense.

---

[8] It does not imply, however, that the firm is enjoying monopoly profits in its business considered as a whole, for (as we shall see shortly) competition to become or remain a monopolist may completely dissipate the profits generated by monopoly pricing. This is consistent, however, with the existence of prices that are monopolistic in the sense that they exceed the competitive price level.

If one asks *how* a firm is able to obtain persistent profits in the economic sense, the normal reply is that the firm has a monopoly, inasmuch as competition would compress price to cost in the long run. The firm may have a monopoly by virtue of conditions that make it the sole or dominant seller in its market and that delay or prevent entry even when the market price is higher than the competitive level (that is, than cost), or by virtue of a price-fixing agreement, explicit or tacit, with its competitors under conditions where entry into the field is delayed or barred. In either case, the creation of monopoly may enable the monopolist to obtain profits in the economic sense—monopoly profits—by reducing output below the competitive level.[9]

Thus the existence of price discrimination is evidence that the seller or sellers engaged in the discrimination have—and are exercising—monopoly power. As we shall see, it is not conclusive evidence of monopoly conduct. But before I explain why this is so, I must explain why a monopolist might wish to discriminate rather than to charge a uniform monopoly price, and why from a social standpoint discrimination might be more objectionable than a uniform monopoly price.

Figure 1 shows the position of the monopolist who charges the single most profitable price given the demand and supply conditions that confront him. The choice of the optimum monopoly price involves locating the rate of output at which marginal revenue equals marginal cost—that is, the output where any increase would add more to the total costs of the firm than to its total revenues (and where reducing output would subtract less from total costs than from total revenues). This point of maximum profitability is reached at output q in Figure 1. The price that clears the market at output q—that is, the price at which purchasers in the aggregate will demand q units—is p. The revenues of the firm are pq and its profits (in the economic sense) are $pq - cq$. Yet p is far from being optimum from the monopolist's standpoint. To the left of p on the demand curve are potential sales at higher prices than p; to the right, potential sales at prices lower than p but higher than c.

What prevents the seller from charging a higher price to the buyers represented by the demand curve above p or a lower price to the buyers who lie along the demand curve between p and the

---

[9] Though, to repeat (see note 8 above), these profits may be transformed into costs through competition to obtain or maintain the monopoly position that generates them.

Figure 1

THE MONOPOLIST WHO CHARGES THE SINGLE MOST PROFITABLE PRICE

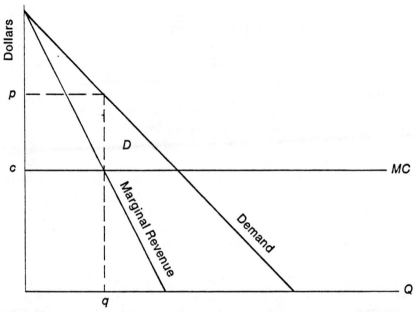

intersection of the demand curve with the cost curve is the effect that charging a higher or lower price would have on his net revenues. If he raised his price, he would be exploiting some consumers more effectively but losing the patronage of others: his gains would be smaller than his losses. Conversely, if he lowered his price, he would be exploiting some customers less effectively while gaining the patronage of others: his gains would still be smaller than his losses. But this assumes that he is constrained to charge a *single* price, the assumption on which we have been proceeding so far. If instead we assume that the seller is able to charge different prices to different buyers, we see that he may be able to increase his net revenues, depending on the costs involved in charging more than a single price for the same good.

Imagine that our seller could, at no cost, identify the intensity of each potential buyer's demand for each unit he might buy and could also, at no cost, prevent any buyer from reselling the good to another buyer. Then the situation would be as depicted in Figure 2. Rather than charging a single price to all buyers, the seller would establish a schedule of different prices, separately calculated for each buyer and for each unit bought by each buyer.

Figure 2
THE PERFECTLY DISCRIMINATING MONOPOLIST

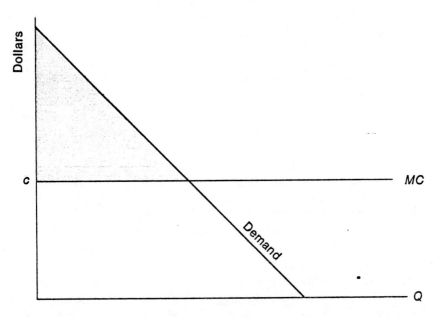

The schedule of prices would coincide with the demand curve between its intersection with the vertical axis and its intersection with the cost curve, and would generate total profits equal to the shaded triangle. A comparison with Figure 1 will reveal that the total profits thus obtained are considerably greater than those under the best single monopoly price.

What would be the economic consequences of perfect price discrimination, the method of pricing depicted in Figure 2? It used to be thought that perfect price discrimination, while perhaps obnoxious on social grounds related to the distribution of income and wealth, was not objectionable on strict economic-efficiency grounds. This conclusion resulted from a traditional view of the monopoly problem that regarded monopoly as inefficient because *and only because* it resulted in a lower output than occurred under competition and a consequent shift of resources to lower-valued goods. Thus, Figure 1 shows that the monopolist sells a smaller quantity of his goods (q) than the firms in a competitive industry would sell. Firms in a competitive industry would carry output to the point where the demand curve intersected the cost curve—that being the point at which the industry's total revenues would just equal its total costs and the price of the product would equal its marginal cost. The reduction in output under monopoly results from substitution by some buyers of other products for those of the monopolist as a result of the monopoly price, and the substitution involves a loss of value. The substitute products must be worth less to the consumer than the monopolized product—otherwise he would have substituted the other products *before* the monopoly price was charged.

Under perfect price discrimination, the output of the monopolist is identical to that of the competitive industry. There is no substitution away from the monopolized product, because the monopolist varies his price in accordance with the intensity of each purchaser's demand; he will not turn away a single sale that he could make at a price higher—however trivially—than his cost of production. Like a competitive industry, the perfectly discriminating monopolist serves the marginal purchaser as well as the purchaser who has an intense demand for his product and who is therefore willing to pay a price higher than cost.

A more recent analysis of the monopoly problem, however, points out that the output, and resulting substitution, effects of monopoly are not the only *and may not be the most important* economic consequence of monopoly pricing. It has been argued that the existence of monopoly profits, or the expectation thereof, will attract resources into the market of the monopolist until at the margin price is equated to cost and the monopolist's return is reduced to a normal level—but by a rise in cost rather than by a decline in price. The resources thus attracted into the monopolizing market are wasted from a social standpoint. They are deadweight costs of monopoly just like the deadweight cost represented by the small triangle (D) in Figure 1.[10]

To illustrate this point, let us suppose that a government regulation fixes the price at which the product represented in Figure 1 may be sold at p but entry into the market is not constrained. Firms will be attracted to the market by the opportunity to obtain the monopoly profits available there. But to get business from existing sellers the new entrants, being forbidden to compete by underpricing those sellers, will seek to differentiate their product in other ways. They will spend heavily on service com-

---

[10] See Richard A. Posner, "The Social Costs of Monopoly and Regulation," *Journal of Political Economy*, vol. 83 (1975) p. 807ff., for an exposition of this approach, which was first suggested in Gordon Tullock, "The Welfare Costs of Tariffs, Monopolies, and Theft," *Western Economic Journal*, vol. 5 (1967), p. 224ff.

petition or make various product improvements. However, these expenditures may greatly exceed the benefits accruing to the consumer from a higher level of service or quality of product. Each seller is not really *selling* the better service or better quality—rather, he is offering it as an inducement to consumers to patronize him rather than his rivals and therefore enable him to obtain the monopoly profit generated by the artificially elevated price. For example, if a particular sale at a normal (that is, a competitive) level of quality or service would yield a monopoly profit of $10, it will pay each seller to spend up to $10 to induce the consumer to buy from him rather than from his competitors. The actual benefit to the consumer from these added expenditures may be much less than $10: a seller might spend $9.99 improving the quality of his service even though his efforts increased the value of the product to the consumer by only two cents, for that two cents might be sufficient to induce the customer to give the seller his patronage—and with it a one cent monopoly profit.

The situation just described is essentially what has prevailed for many years in the airline industry.[11] It cannot be determined with accuracy how great is the deadweight cost of nonprice competition designed to engross the monopoly profits generated by a price fixed above the competitive level. It is probably not so great as $pq - cq$ in Figure 1 because, as noted, expenditures on nonprice competition generate some benefits for consumers. But the social loss might be a large fraction of that rectangle. It might greatly exceed the triangle (D in Figure 1) that is the normal measure of the social cost of monopoly and is, as we have seen, completely eliminated under perfect price discrimination.

Where, rather than the government, a cartel or a single firm having monopoly power fixes the supracompetitive price, the analysis becomes somewhat more complex. In particular, as is not the case with government regulation, a newcomer to the industry is free to underprice the existing firms, and if new competition assumes that particular form it is not costly in the sense just described. However, while the entry of price cutters will eventually, at low social cost, eliminate the monopoly pricing and profits of the firms in the market, there may be an interval before such entry occurs on a scale large enough to eliminate the monopoly power of the existing firms in the market. Indeed,

---

[11] George W. Douglas and James C. Miller III, *Economic Regulation of Domestic Air Transport* (Washington, D.C.: The Brookings Institution, 1974).

unless there is such an interval, monopoly pricing will be infeasible in the first place and the problem of monopoly will not arise.

To the extent that the entry of the price cutters is delayed, monopoly profits will be available to the industry for a time. Firms will have an incentive to try to engross as large a share of the expected profits as they can by engaging in various (and costly) forms of nonprice competition. Moreover, anticipating the profits that monopolization might yield, firms will expend real resources on forming or entering cartels or otherwise creating monopoly, including an expenditure of resources on trying to persuade the government to confer a legal monopoly or bring about equivalent conditions through various forms of regulation. Thus the costs of monopoly that result from efforts to obtain monopoly—as distinct from the costs that result from the reduced output of the monopolist—remain a strong objection to monopoly pricing in the unregulated sector as well.

Deadweight Loss from Systematic Price Discrimination. In the foregoing perspective, perfect price discrimination is seen as aggravating rather than alleviating the monopoly problem. Although it eliminates the costs that result from the reduced output of the monopolist, it is likely to increase the costs that result from efforts to obtain or share in a monopoly. By increasing the expected gains from monopolizing a market, and thereby making monopolizing a more profitable activity than if a single price were charged, perfect price discrimination increases the incentive to monopolize and hence is likely to increase the expenditures made on obtaining monopolies.[12] These expenditures represent a deadweight social cost that may, as we have seen, exceed the social costs conventionally associated with monopoly pricing.

It may be objected that perfect price discrimination is only a theoretical construct: this is true, but it does not weaken the analysis. The costs of identifying the individual intensities of demand of particular purchasers for particular quantities are considerable, which means that price discrimination in actual practice, even when not inhibited by the threat of legal action, will invariably take much cruder forms than suggested by Figure 2. Rather than negotiating separately with every purchaser on every sale, the discriminating seller will divide his potential customers into fairly gross categories and charge the same price to everyone within each category. Youth fares, excursion fares,

---

[12] See Posner, "The Social Costs of Monopoly and Regulation," p. 822.

and family plans in the airline industry are examples of the crude price categories used by discriminating sellers faced by real-world cost constraints.

Another complication involved in carrying out price discrimination is the cost of keeping buyers who have been placed in different price categories from trading with one another. Such trading, called arbitrage, can utterly destroy an attempt at price discrimination. Customers finding themselves in the lowest-price category simply increase their purchases until they are taking the seller's entire output, which they then resell to other purchasers at higher prices—until arbitrage does these sellers in too.

From a social standpoint, the limited, crude, and costly methods of price discrimination that one encounters in practice are both worse and better than perfect price discrimination. Imperfect discrimination is better in that the profits of the imperfectly discriminating seller are lower than those of the perfect discriminator, both because the costs to the former of implementing the discriminatory scheme are higher and because the scheme is less effective in extracting the last bit of consumer surplus from every buyer. The social costs of monopoly that arise from the tendency to transform monopoly profits into resource costs will therefore be smaller with imperfect than with perfect discrimination. Imperfect discrimination is worse, however, in that it does not have the beneficent effect that perfect price discrimination would have on the output of the monopolist. In fact, it can be shown that under conditions of imperfect price discrimination, output may be smaller than under single price monopoly.[13] In short, the substitution effects of imperfectly discriminating monopoly are expected on average to be no worse (and no better) than those of nondiscriminating monopoly; in the output effects of monopoly, there is a "wash." But the imperfectly discriminating monopoly is worse than the nondiscriminating monopoly from the point of view of the resource costs of monopoly, since the profits of the discriminating monopoly, while lower than those of the *perfectly* discriminating monopolist, are nonetheless higher than those of the nondiscriminating monopolist (otherwise a monopolist would not bother to discriminate). Hence the amount of resources likely to be invested in attempting to obtain and hold monopoly positions will be greater under discriminating than under single-price monopoly.

---

[13] See Richard A. Posner, *Antitrust Law: An Economic Perspective* (Chicago: University of Chicago Press, 1976), p. 64, and references cited there.

An important caveat should be entered at this point. The analysis assumes that expenditures on monopolizing activities are not socially valued beyond the immediate benefits (in better service, for example) they provide to the buyer of the monopolized product. But they may be: in particular, society may wish to use monopoly pricing as a device for inducing a greater expenditure on innovation than would otherwise be forthcoming. In that case, the social objection to price discrimination based on its effect in inducing greater expenditures on monopolizing disappears. The principal example, however, appears to be price discrimination by patentees and has, as we shall see, only a limited relevance to the enforcement of the Robinson-Patman Act.

Persistent Discrimination and Sporadic Discrimination. To summarize the discussion to this point, there is a substantial objection to unrestricted price discrimination on strictly economic grounds even if one ignores the point made at the outset—a substantial point, I might add—about the possible distorting effects of discrimination on competition between customers forced to pay different prices for the same input. Inefficiencies are created in the sellers' market as well. However, before concluding that price discrimination should be banned because of the economic objections to it, we must be careful to note a fundamental distinction between merely sporadic or temporary discrimination on the one hand and systematic or persistent discrimination on the other. I have here been discussing discrimination of the latter sort. It is the sort of discrimination that indeed cannot be explained other than in terms of possession of monopoly power, so that unless we approve the particular instance of monopoly power we can have no kind words for discrimination. But discrimination of the temporary or sporadic sort is by no means a practice limited to monopolists, and forbidding it could actually reinforce monopoly as well as producing other economic distortions.

To grasp this point, it is first necessary to understand in a general way the economic concept of long-run equilibrium. This can be defined as a stable situation in which firms have had a chance to adjust to the last change that has occurred in the conditions of demand or supply. This stability is only occasionally attained in the real world. Firms are faced with constant changes in their environment, and the process of adapting to those changes and reaching equilibrium is time-consuming rather than instantaneous. Indeed, it is possible for a firm never actually to reach equilibrium, but always to be merely tending toward it, because the firm is constantly beset with shocks to which it must adapt and can never finish adapting to one wave of shocks before it is hit by a new wave. Price discrimination is likely to accompany the transition from one equilibrium to another, that is, the adjustment to external shocks, and indeed to facilitate that transition.

Let us suppose that a firm is selling the identical product in two different areas separated by high transport costs, and there is an unexpected surge in demand for its product in one area. To increase its output in that area, the firm must increase production there, which will take some time. Meanwhile it will raise its price in that area as a means of rationing a supply which has suddenly become short in relation to the newly increased demand. The resulting price increase will create at least an apparent discrimination [14] because the same product, having the same long-run production cost, will continue to be sold in the other market area at a lower price.[15] Eventually, these prices will be equalized as the seller (or some other seller) increases output in the market where demand has suddenly risen and prices fall accordingly.[16] The process of adjustment would be inhibited rather than facilitated by forbidding the temporary "discrimination."

Now let us assume that firms in the high-price area in the foregoing example begin to construct additional capacity so as to be able to meet the increased demand in the area. As a firm's added capacity becomes ready to operate, the firm will seek additional customers to make use of that capacity (additions to capacity being inevitably lumpy and therefore at the time they are made somewhat in excess of any additional business available from current customers). The firm finds the customers of other firms (on which the customers have learned to rely) unwilling to switch unless offered some inducement. It therefore offers a price cut and the prospective customer finds its usual supplier un-

---

[14] See note 15 below.

[15] Technically speaking, however, there is no price discrimination in the economic sense, because the short-run marginal cost in the high-price area is higher than the short-run marginal cost in the low-price area, as a result of the difficulty of increasing output in the former area on short notice, and the price will (assuming competition) be equal to that cost.

[16] Of course, the unit cost of supplying the market with a higher output may exceed the cost of supplying a smaller output in the firm's other markets. Then the prices will not be equalized. But the consequent difference will not be discriminatory in the economic sense, because it will reflect a cost difference.

believing when informed that a rival has offered a lower price (since everyone has been straining capacity, why would anyone cut?), and refuses to meet the cut. The customer switches suppliers. The new supplier is now discriminating between its regular (old) customers and its new customer, selling to the latter at a lower price. If it had to cut price to everyone to get this new customer, the price would not be cut.

The former supplier of the detached customer now has excess capacity, having lost a buyer to his competitor, and seeks a replacement. He, in turn, manages to detach a customer from some other firm (or from this one) with a lower price offer. Thus the discrimination spreads through the market until there is no longer any discrimination because everyone comes to be served at the lower price (sufficient additional capacity having come on stream to provide for increased demand at the lower price). Sporadic price discrimination has moved this market to its new long-run equilibrium position much more quickly than reluctant, delayed, across-the-board price cuts would have done.

Many other examples of beneficial discrimination could be given—like that of the firm which, because it has declining average costs over the relevant range of output, cannot maximize its output by selling at a uniform price—but I shall skip over these and come immediately to a kind of transitional price discrimination particularly relevant in the present context. This is the kind of discrimination that occurs in a market that is already monopolized. Let us suppose that the sellers in a market have formed a cartel and agreed on a cartel price. (I shall assume a single cartel price but the analysis would not be changed essentially—it would only be made more complicated—if a discriminatory price schedule were assumed.) Let us suppose one of the sellers decides that he could make more money if he shaded the cartel price. He knows that if he made an across-the-board price cut his defection from the cartel agreement would be discovered and the other sellers would lower their prices, with the result that his gains from cheating would be reduced or eliminated. Instead he decides to grant only selected discounts—probably to the larger buyers, for that way he can obtain a large profit per customer while minimizing the risk of detection by minimizing the number of customers with whom he is dealing on a cut price basis.[17] This sort of cheating has a tendency to spread. Many cartels have

---

[17] See George J. Stigler, "A Theory of Oligopoly," in Stigler, *The Organization of Industry* (Homewood, Ill.: Richard D. Irwin, 1968), pp. 39 and 43-44.

collapsed as a result of the progressive deterioration of the cartel price structure caused by discriminatory price reductions. The railroad cartels of the nineteenth century were apparently highly unstable as a result of the opportunities that existed for discriminatory price reductions. This was one of the reasons that the first Interstate Commerce Act (a statute mainly designed to prevent price discrimination) was passed in 1887, apparently with the connivance of the railroads.[18]

The short of it is that an effectively enforced across-the-board prohibition of price discrimination would have a serious—perhaps disastrous—impact on the ability of industries to adapt efficiently to changing circumstances, and in particular on the natural tendency of cartels to collapse through cheating that typically begins with discriminatory reductions. This transitional or temporary or sporadic discrimination is conceptually distinct from the systematic, persistent discrimination practiced by a monopolist or cartel; the problem is to distinguish these practices in the real world, using the inevitably crude methods of administrative and judicial fact finding. I have argued elsewhere that the difficulties of making the distinction may not be insuperable in all cases, and that an economically oriented program designed to prevent collusive pricing would rely in part on evidence of systematic discrimination, and hence would implicitly distinguish between that and the sporadic form.[19] It is a separate question whether the law should attempt to prohibit systematic price discrimination directly. It is still another question, as we shall see, whether the Robinson-Patman Act is an apt vehicle for implementing such a prohibition. But contrary to some students of competition and monopoly, I do not regard concern with the economic consequences of price discrimination as misplaced. The problem is one of translating this concern into sound and workable public policy.

Noneconomic Objections to Price Discrimination and to Non-discriminatory Price Differences. It remains for us to consider whether there may not be justifications for a law limiting dis-

---

[18] See George W. Hilton, "The Consistency of the Interstate Commerce Act," *Journal of Law and Economics*, vol. 9 (1966), p. 87; Gabriel Kolko, *Railroads and Regulation, 1877-1916* (Princeton: Princeton University Press, 1965); Paul W. MacAvoy, *The Economic Effects of Regulation: The Trunk-Line Railroad Cartels and the Interstate Commerce Commission before 1900* (Cambridge, Mass.: M.I.T. Press, 1965).

[19] See Posner, *Antitrust Law: An Economic Perspective*, pp. 62-65.

criminatory or differential pricing that have nothing to do with the economist's objection to price discrimination. In general, as we shall see, the thrust of the Robinson-Patman Act has been to limit price differences that tend to favor certain purchasers, even if the price differences are economically justified and are not the result of price discrimination, whether persistent or sporadic. If the purchasers thereby protected by the state represented "small business," or some coherent, identifiable subcategory of small businessmen, as some supporters of the act believe, I would have to consider the case for protecting small business from more efficient big business. I would still try to avoid having to answer the ultimate question of social policy by pointing out that, even if it were deemed desirable to protect small business, to do so by trying to limit price cuts given to competing big businesses would be an oblique, very costly, and probably ineffective method. A lower tax rate on small firms, for example, would probably be a preferable means for accomplishing this objective.

In general, price differences involving a specific input are not likely to be an important factor in the survival of a firm. And quite often when there are potential purchasing economies or other factors that might lead to such price differences, small firms can organize in various ways to obtain the same advantages enjoyed by large firms: a purchasing cooperative of small firms is one example. We shall see that small-business purchasing cooperatives have been a favorite target of Robinson-Patman enforcement, which raises a second objection to a small-business rationale for the Robinson-Patman Act: the act as enforced has not in fact "discriminated" effectively in favor of small business. Some small businesses are probably helped by the act—how else can we explain why it has not been repealed yet?—but they represent a small and arbitrary subset of the arguably deserving small businesses, and one practically limited, moreover, to the distribution industries.[20] In the absence of any comparable policies favoring small businesses in other industries, the importance of the act in some general scheme favoring small business may be doubted.

I shall not consider the small-business question further here but shall return to the question in discussing the specific enforcement of the act, where it will be seen that as enforced the act has never meant much to small businesses in general and that it is unlikely that it could be transformed into an effective instrument

---

[20] See p. 37 below.

of small-business promotion. There is accordingly no occasion for me to reach in this study the ultimate question whether public policy should favor small business.

Having discussed various social objectives to which a price discrimination law might be thought pertinent, I shall turn in the next section to a brief review of the antecedents, provisions, and enforcement history of the Robinson-Patman Act.

II. THE HISTORY OF THE ROBINSON-PATMAN ACT AND ITS ENFORCEMENT

The roots of the Robinson-Patman Act of 1936 lie in the late nineteenth century, the era of the great "trusts"—the monopolies and cartels that were formed in the period roughly between 1875 and 1905. The best known of these was John D. Rockefeller's Standard Oil Trust, eventually challenged under section 2 of the Sherman Act. In 1911 the Supreme Court affirmed the judgment of the trial court ordering the dissolution of the trust.[21]

Economic Characteristics of the Practices of the Standard Oil Trust. Among the many misdeeds the Standard Oil Trust was alleged to have committed, two bore in particular on the issues that were later to be addressed by the framers of the Robinson-Patman Act. First, Standard Oil was alleged to have engaged in the practice known as "area price discrimination" or "local price cutting." This is the practice of a firm that, having monopoly power in one market, lowers its price in some other market where it faces competition (or the threat of competition) to whatever level is necessary to eliminate the competitor (or the competitive threat), even if that level is below cost. This practice would later be referred to as "primary-line discrimination" because the intended impact is felt at the level of distribution at which the discriminating seller operates. It is a device whereby that seller eliminates his competition.

The second allegation against the Standard Oil Trust that is relevant here was that the trust was receiving secret rebates from railroads. Standard was thought to owe its rise to a monopoly position—and its continued possession of that position—in part to its ability to extract secret discounts from the railroads that

---

[21] See Standard Oil Co. of New Jersey v. United States, 221 U.S. 1 (1911).

transported its oil to market—these secret discounts being in the form of rebates that were denied the competitors of Standard, thereby raising their costs relative to those of Standard. It was further alleged that these rebates reflected not any lower costs of selling to Standard but simply the economic muscle of the trust.[22]

The practice of receiving discounts denied competitors was later to be known as "secondary-line discrimination" because the injury occurred not to competitors of the discriminating seller but to buyers who were in competition with the recipients of the lower price. The concern in the *Standard Oil* case was not with competition among railroads but with the impact on competition in the oil industry of Standard's alleged ability to extract discriminatory rebates from its suppliers of railroad services.

These allegations raised two questions. The first was whether the practices in question ought to be forbidden; the second was whether they were forbidden by the existing antitrust laws (which at the time of the *Standard Oil* case meant the Sherman Act). In answering the first question, it is necessary to distinguish between primary-line and secondary-line discrimination—that is, area discrimination and rebates—because they raise different issues. A great debate has raged over the questions whether and in what circumstances selling below cost is a rational method of obtaining or maintaining monopoly power and whether and in what circumstances it is a method with which the law should be concerned.[23] An important article by John McGee, based on a careful study of the trial record in the *Standard Oil* case, found no substantial evidence that Standard had in fact engaged in predatory pricing.[24] Later writers on the question (I am included among them), while not denying McGee's major point—that it was cheaper for Standard to purchase competitors than to drive them out of business by selling below cost—have pointed out that, in

---

[22] On Standard's rebates see E. A. G. Robinson, *Monopoly* (London: James Nisbet and Co., 1941), pp. 199-202.

[23] See B. S. Yamey, "Predatory Price Cutting: Notes and Comments," *Journal of Law and Economics*, vol. 15 (1972), p. 129ff., and references cited there (reprinted in Yale Brozen, ed., *The Competitive Economy: Selected Readings* [Morristown, N.J.: General Learning Press, 1975]). For a recent contribution see Roland H. Koller, "The Myth of Predatory Pricing: An Empirical Survey," *Antitrust Law and Economics Review*, vol. 4 (1971), p. 105ff. (reprinted in Brozen, *Competitive Economy*).

[24] John S. McGee, "Predatory Price Cutting: The Standard Oil (N.J.) Case," *Journal of Law and Economics*, vol. 1 (1958), p. 137ff. (reprinted in Brozen, *Competitive Economy*).

some circumstances at least, below-cost pricing is a rational method of obtaining or maintaining a monopoly; and where those circumstances are present, the threat alone, even an implicit threat, may be sufficient to accomplish the seller's predatory aims while leaving no traces in a trial record. In particular, it has been pointed out that a firm operating in many more markets than its actual or potential competitors may be able to make credible threats to engage in below-cost pricing in individual markets where competition rears its head.[25] Standard Oil was such a firm, although that does not mean it actually made such threats.[26] Nevertheless, the danger that a firm so situated might do so is sufficient to persuade me to favor (at least tentatively) the prohibition of "predatory pricing," properly defined as selling below cost with intent to eliminate a competitor.[27]

But the objection to predatory pricing, although a substantial one, has no intrinsic connection with public policy on price discrimination. That a firm selling below cost in one market may be charging a higher price for the same goods in another market, and thus engaging in price discrimination, is a detail in the analysis of predatory pricing. The objection to predatory pricing is an objection to selling at uneconomically low prices with the purpose of driving out of business what may be equally or even more efficient firms: what the predatory seller may be doing in another market is irrelevant. True, the higher price in the other market (by assumption a price above cost [28]) may generate profits that the predator could use to finance his below-cost selling. But the possession of funds does not dictate the use to which they will be put. Unless below-cost selling is a profitable activity, the monopolist will not expend funds in its pursuit; and if it is a profitable activity, he should have no difficulty in raising funds to pursue it.[29]

I want to emphasize that so long as the lower of the two prices being charged by the alleged predator is higher than his cost, properly defined, the fact that he is discriminating does not imply that the lower price is predatory. A price that exceeds the

---

[25] See Posner, *Antitrust Law: An Economic Perspective*, pp. 185-87.

[26] As noted below, neither court that decided the *Standard Oil* case found it necessary to decide whether Standard had in fact either engaged in predatory pricing or received railroad rebates.

[27] See Posner, *Antitrust Law: An Economic Perspective*, pp. 188-93.

[28] See p. 4 above.

[29] See George J. Stigler, "Imperfections in the Capital Market," in Stigler, *The Organization of Industry*, p. 113ff.

seller's cost cannot exclude an equally or more efficient competitor and hence is unobjectionable from an economic standpoint, and it does not become objectionable merely because the seller is charging a higher price in some other market. Discrimination may be objectionable on economic grounds, as argued in Section I of this study, but not because the price charged to favored purchasers harms competitors of the discriminating seller. So long as that price exceeds the seller's costs, it cannot be attacked as inefficiently low—that is, as being calculated to drive out of the market an equally or more efficient competitor. Price discrimination, in short, is neither a necessary nor a sufficient condition for condemning the charging of low prices on the ground that those prices are predatory.

On the question of secondary-line discrimination—such as the alleged receipt of discriminatory rebates by the Standard Oil Trust—it is true, as pointed out in Section I of this study, that if a firm is able to buy inputs at a lower price than that charged competing firms, and the difference is not justified by a difference between the cost of supplying the favored firm and the cost of supplying its competitors, the favored firm will enjoy a competitive advantage unrelated to efficiency. But it is necessary to go a step further and ask how it is that a firm could extract such favored treatment from its suppliers. There are two possible answers. The first is that the buying firm has what is called monopsony power—the power of a firm, by reducing the amount of an input that it purchases, to force the price of that input below the competitive level.[30] The process is illustrated in Figure 3, in which, by reducing its purchase of the input from q_c to q_m, the buyer is able to equate its marginal cost of the input with the marginal gain it derives from the input, and thus reduce its costs of production.

But even if a buyer is the sole buyer of the particular input, he may not have monopsony power. Since an industry in which the firms do not obtain a normal return on their investment will cease to reinvest and will gradually phase out its operations, the buyer who attempts to exploit a monopsony position by depressing an input price below its competitive level may find that he has destroyed the industry on which he depends for the input. To be sure, if the producing industry utilizes resources that are (1) durable and (2) immobile (in the sense that they cannot be shifted to other industries without losing much of their value), the

---

[30] See Stigler, *Theory of Price*, pp. 205-7.

Figure 3
THE BUYER WHO IS A MONOPSONIST

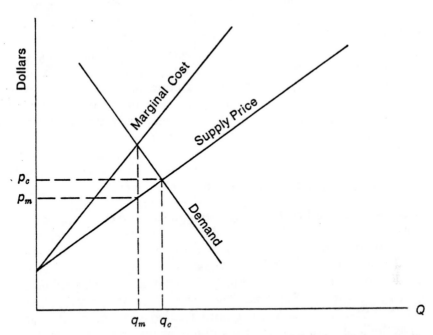

process of disinvestment may proceed very slowly and it may be many years before the industry ceases production through the deterioration and nonreplacement of its productive assets caused by its inability to obtain an adequate return on its investment. But since it is unlikely that these conditions are commonly satisfied, it would appear that "monopsonizing" poses only a small danger to the efficient functioning of the economy. Reasonably well documented cases of monopsony are rare.

The other (and much the more probable) explanation for the rebates allegedly involved in the *Standard Oil* case is that Standard Oil was exploiting the weakness of the railroad cartels. It is now well established that the railroads in the late nineteenth century did practice cartelization on a large scale, but with only mixed success owing to the propensity of individual railroads to cheat on their fellow cartelists.[31] For reasons explained in Section I of this study, this cheating often took the form of secret discounts or rebates to large customers, and Standard Oil was one of the largest. If this is the correct explanation of the rebates

---

[31] See references in note 17 above.

that Standard received, those rebates were not cost-justified and they created between Standard and its competitors a disparity in input costs that was unrelated to any superior efficiency on Standard's part. But to have forbidden the rebates would have strengthened the railroad cartels by making it more difficult for railroads to cheat on their fellow cartelists without being discovered, which is why the railroad industry was happy to have rebates outlawed by the Interstate Commerce Act. One way—perhaps the only way—to have avoided this dilemma would have been for the government to proceed vigorously under antitrust law against the railroad cartels. If the cartels had been destroyed, both their ability to practice systematic discrimination and their temptation to engage in sporadic discrimination as a way of cheating on a cartel price would have been eliminated.

Legality of These Practices under the Sherman Act. The Supreme Court in the *Standard Oil* case did not discuss either area price discrimination or rebates as specific illegal acts by the Standard Oil Trust. Although both practices were alleged in the government's complaint and the subject of evidence at trial, neither the trial court nor the Supreme Court found it necessary to decide whether Standard Oil had committed either practice or, if it had, what the legal significance of the practices was.[32] The illegality of the trust was determined on different grounds.

In retrospect, it is clear that the courts could have saved Congress a great deal of trouble had they indicated that the alleged discriminatory practices, if in fact committed by Standard, would have violated the Sherman Act. The Supreme Court might, for example, have said that predatory pricing, being an inefficient and exclusionary practice, was an act of illegal monopolization under section 2 of the Sherman Act when it was engaged in by a firm already enjoying monopoly power or obtaining it by means of the predatory pricing.[33] Or the Court might even have said that the sale of goods below cost with intent to exclude a competitor was an unreasonable contract or combination in restraint of trade between the seller and the favored purchasers and hence a violation of section 1 of the Sherman Act. On the question of the railroad rebates, the Court might have said that the practice of a

---

[32] See United States v. Standard Oil Co., 173 Fed. 177, 192 (Cir. Ct. E.D. Mo. 1909).

[33] Even in the absence of monopoly power, predatory pricing could be deemed unlawful as an attempt to monopolize (also forbidden by section 2) if the pricing created a dangerous probability of monopolization.

monopolist in obtaining non-cost-justified rebates giving it an unfair advantage over its actual or potential competitors was also an act of illegal monopolization under section 2, or alternatively that the granting of the rebates created a contract or combination in restraint of trade between the recipient and the grantor, in violation of section 1.

I do not mean that the courts acted improperly in "ducking" these issues, given the considerable doubt whether Standard Oil had, in fact, engaged in the alleged practices and the existence of alternative grounds for deciding the case. The point is, rather, that by failing to condemn the specific abuses in which Standard Oil was widely believed to have engaged, the courts created (perhaps unjustifiable) doubts whether the existing law was adequate to curb these abuses.

Section 2 of the Original Clayton Act. Dissatisfaction with the Supreme Court's opinion in the *Standard Oil* case was apparently a major factor in the enactment three years later of the Clayton Act and the Federal Trade Commission Act.[34] A principal purpose of both statutes was to suppress specific anticompetitive practices of the kind that Standard Oil and other trusts were alleged to have engaged in but the illegality of which had been left unclear by the *Standard Oil* decision. One of the practices was price discrimination; section 2 of the Clayton Act forbade the charging of discriminatory prices where the effect might be to lessen competition substantially.[35] The purpose of this provision

---

[34] See Gerard C. Henderson, *The Federal Trade Commission* (Washington, D.C.: The Brookings Institution, 1924), Chapter 1.

[35] The full text of section 2, 38 Stat. 730, is as follows:

That it shall be unlawful for any person engaged in commerce, in the course of such commerce, either directly or indirectly, to discriminate in price between different purchasers of commodities, which commodities are sold for use, consumption, or resale within the United States or any Territory thereof or the District of Columbia or any insular possession or other place under the jurisdiction of the United States, where the effect of such discrimination may be to substantially lessen competition or tend to create a monopoly in any line of commerce: *Provided*, That nothing herein contained shall prevent discrimination in price between purchasers of commodities on account of differences in the grade, quality, or quantity of the commodity sold, or that makes only due allowance for differences in the cost of selling or transportation, or discrimination in price in the same or different communities made in good faith to meet competition: *And provided further*, That nothing herein contained shall prevent persons engaged in selling goods, wares, or merchandise in commerce from selling their own customers in bona fide transactions and not in restraint of trade.

was to forbid the kinds of price discrimination, including both area price discrimination and receipt of railroad rebates, in which Standard Oil had allegedly been involved,[36] and the language of the provision was plainly broad enough to embrace both primary-line and secondary-line discrimination—that is, discrimination whether harmful to competing sellers or to buyers. Moreover, the draftsmen apparently believed that they were attenuating the Sherman Act requirement of proving anticompetitive effect. In a proceeding under section 2 of the Clayton Act, the plaintiff, instead of having to prove an actual restraint of trade, had only to prove that the challenged practice might substantially lessen competition. Although the difference between the Sherman Act and Clayton Act tests of competitive effect is more semantic than real,[37] there can be no question that Congress—in section 2 as in the other provisions of the Clayton Act and in the Federal Trade Commission Act—was inviting the courts and the newly created commission to suppress any discriminatory practice that was substantially anticompetitive. In short, the courts and the agency were given a broad mandate to extirpate the practices alleged in the *Standard Oil* case.

The antitrust legislation of 1914—the Clayton and Federal Trade Commission acts—constitutes one of the great failures of legislative reform. The notions of singling out particular competitive practices for condemnation and of creating an administrative agency for antitrust administration seem to have been fundamentally unsound in ways even today not fully understood. With unerring aim the Congress struck at practices that were unimportant in the growth of monopolies. Section 3 of the Clayton Act forbade anticompetitive tie-in and exclusive-dealing contracts, and it is fairly clear that neither of these practices has ever contributed substantially to the creation of monopoly power.[38] Section 7 of the act forbade certain *stock* acquisitions, and by thus failing to include mergers (a form of asset acquisition) was easily evaded and essentially of no importance until the statute was thoroughly overhauled in 1950 by the Celler-Kefauver Antimerger Act.[39] Section 8 of the Clayton Act dealt with interlocking directorates which, it is now clear, have never

---

[36] See Henderson, *The Federal Trade Commission*, pp. 28-30.

[37] See Posner, *Antitrust Law: An Economic Perspective*, pp. 212-14.

[38] Ibid., Chapter 8.

[39] This story is told· in United States v. Philadelphia National Bank, 374 U.S. 321, 334-40 (1963).

been an important factor in monopolizing or cartelizing.[40] Section 5 of the Federal Trade Commission Act empowered the commission to define and prevent "unfair methods of competition," but in practice these turned out to be Sherman and Clayton act violations (with occasional forays into practices either innocuous or trivial from a competitive standpoint), along with false advertising.[41]

The remaining substantive provision in the Clayton and Federal Trade Commission acts of 1914 was section 2 of the Clayton Act, and in its administration it proved an immense disappointment to its supporters. Early decisions held that the statute had no application to discrimination challenged as harmful to competition at the buyer level (that is, secondary-line discrimination),[42] but these decisions were later overruled.[43] More seriously, the statutory exemption for price differences made on account of quantity differences[44] was held to provide a blanket immunity for quantity discounts.[45] Still, the Sherman Act remained available to deal with both primary-line and secondary-line price discrimination that produced substantial anticompetitive effects. The fact that the Sherman Act, as supplemented by section 2 of the Clayton Act, had little impact suggests above all that price discrimination may never have been an important factor in the creation or perpetuation of monopoly conditions.

The Passage of the Robinson-Patman Act. The depression of the 1930s created all sorts of demands for government assistance to businessmen. Moreover, this was the era of rapid growth for chain stores such as A&P, which were able *inter alia* to exploit efficiencies in centralized purchasing of food, groceries, and other consumer products. The growth of the chains placed great competitive pressure on various other firms engaged in distribution,

---

[40] See George J. Stigler, "The Economic Effects of the Antitrust Laws," in Stigler, *The Organization of Industry,* pp. 259-61.

[41] For my general views on the FTC see Richard A. Posner, "The Federal Trade Commission," *University of Chicago Law Review,* vol. 37 (1969), p. 47ff. See also Posner, *Regulation of Advertising by the FTC* (Washington, D.C.: American Enterprise Institute, 1973).

[42] See National Biscuit Co. v. FTC, 299 Fed. 733 (2d Cir. 1924); Mennen Co. v. FTC, 288 Fed. 774 (2d Cir. 1923).

[43] See George Van Camp & Sons Co. v. American Can Co., 278 U.S. 245 (1929).

[44] See note 35 above.

[45] Goodyear Tire & Rubber Co. v. FTC, 101 F.2d 620 (6th Cir. 1939), setting aside 22 FTC 232 (1936). Although the *Goodyear* decision actually postdates the enactment of the Robinson-Patman Act, it had long been anticipated on the basis of the statutory language relating to quantity discounts.

including food brokers, retail groceries, and retail drug stores that were not themselves organized into chains. A&P, which in this period enjoyed much the same symbolic status as Standard Oil had enjoyed in an earlier trust-busting era, was accused of obtaining discriminatory advantages from its suppliers, both directly, by being charged lower prices, and indirectly, by receiving spurious brokerage and advertising allowances that constituted covert price reductions denied its competitors. In many states hostility to chains led to the enactment of anti-chain-store legislation.[46] The movement against the chains was worldwide, and hostility to chain stores was a tenet of Nazi economic policy in this period.[47]

There is grave doubt that the charges of anticompetitive conduct leveled against the chains were true. The ease of entry into the retail drug and grocery markets and other sectors of distribution makes it unlikely that a firm could obtain monopoly power in any branch of distribution, so it is not surprising that no responsible evidence of widespread monopoly abuses in distribution, in the 1930s or at any other time, has ever been presented. It is especially noteworthy that the Federal Trade Commission's exhaustive study of chain-store practices, the study that was ostensibly behind the Robinson-Patman Act, largely exonerated the chains from the charges of wrongdoing that had been leveled against them.[48]

Nonetheless, the act, the high-water mark of the anti-chain-store movement, was passed by Congress in 1936.[49] The provisions of the act will be examined in some detail in the next section of this study: for our purposes in this section, a brief summary of the changes made by the new law will suffice.

Former section 2 of the Clayton Act became subsection (a) of an expanded section 2. This new section 2(a) differed from the old section 2 primarily in the following respects: it added a new test of anticompetitive effect, designed to attenuate still further the statutory requirement of proving competitive injury; it closed

---

[46] The history of the anti-chain-store movement is summarized in Frederick M. Rowe, *Price Discrimination under the Robinson-Patman Act* (Boston: Little, Brown and Co., 1962), pp. 8-11.

[47] See Arthur Schweitzer, *Big Business in the Third Reich* (Bloomington, Ind.: Indiana University Press, 1964), pp. 85, 114, 117-22.

[48] See FTC, *Final Report on the Chain Store Investigation*, Senate Document No. 7, 74th Congress, 1st session (1935), discussed in Rowe, *Price Discrimination under the Robinson-Patman Act*, pp. 9-10.

[49] See note 1 above.

the quantity-discount loophole and tightened the cost-justification defense; and it narrowed the meeting-competition defense and moved it to a new subsection (b).

Subsections (c) through (e) of the amended section 2 were completely new prohibitions, added by the Robinson-Patman Act. In them, the act's framers resorted to the old Clayton Act technique of singling out for special condemnation practices thought to be especially wicked, in this case certain brokerage payments and advertising allowances and facilities. Subsection (f), also added by the Robinson-Patman Act, forbade the knowing inducement of an illegal discrimination by the buyer.

In addition to amending section 2 of the Clayton Act, the Robinson-Patman Act, in its section 3, created several new criminal offenses—in particular, that of selling at unreasonably low prices with intent to destroy competition.[50] Fortunately, this has been interpreted to mean below-cost, predatory pricing.[51] Because section 3 of the Robinson-Patman Act has been so rarely invoked, I shall not discuss it further in this study.

The great question raised by the history and language of the Robinson-Patman Act is the extent to which Congress wanted not merely to provide more effective regulation of the types of price discrimination that are inefficient or anticompetitive in some legitimate economic sense, but also (or instead) to prevent price differences that—regardless of their possible justifications on grounds of efficiency—might be injurious to segments of the business community that were influential in the enactment of the legislation. I regard this question as largely unanswerable. One can find in the legislative history of the Robinson-Patman Act many indications of a hostility to chain stores apparently unrelated to any coherent belief that the chain stores' advantages were due to monopolistic practices in some plausible economic sense of the term *monopoly*.[52] Yet even the most incoherent diatribes against the chain stores sought support from the policy against monopoly, as in the following remarks of co-sponsor Wright Patman:

> This bill has the opposition of all cheaters, chiselers, bribe takers, bribe givers, and the greedy who seek

---

[50] 15 U.S.C., sec. 13a.

[51] See, for example, United States v. National Dairy Products Co., 372 U.S. 29 (1963).

[52] The legislative history of the act is summarized in Rowe, *Price Discrimination under the Robinson-Patman Act*, pp. 11-23.

monopolistic powers which would destroy opportunity for all young people and which would eventually cause Government ownership, as the people of this country will not tolerate private monopoly.

This bill has the support of those who believe that competition is the life of trade; that the policy of live and let live is a good one; that it is one of the first duties of Government to protect the weak against the strong and prevent men from injuring one another; that greed should be restrained and the Golden Rule practiced.[53]

Moreover, even if passages such as these should be interpreted as indicating support for a noneconomic policy against chain stores, one cannot be sure that such passages represent the sentiment of a majority of Congress. It is easy for those congressmen who wish to influence the interpretation of legislation to fill the *Congressional Record* with personal views of the meaning of the legislation that may be unrepresentative of the views of the "silent majority" of congressmen. The committee reports, which are generally regarded as a more authoritative expression of congressional opinion than the floor debates, are in the case of the Robinson-Patman Act much more guarded than the floor debates, and can be read as being concerned primarily with alleged monopoly abuses by A&P and other firms.[54] Moreover, the act that emerged continued to speak in terms of competition rather than of the promotion of inefficient non-chain enterprises.

At the same time, however, it is plain that Congress was dissatisfied with the old section 2 of the Clayton Act, and not merely with the quantity-discount loophole in that section; and it seems difficult to believe that all Congress thought it was doing in the Robinson-Patman Act was reaffirming the Clayton Act's policy of preventing monopoly. Furthermore, by 1936 it was reasonably clear that the kinds of practices in which the Standard Oil Company had engaged were unlawful either under the Sherman Act or the old section 2 of the Clayton Act (or more probably under both), so there was little basis for doubting that public policy, as expressed in existing antitrust legislation, was firmly against genuinely anticompetitive price differences, making a statute limited to such differences redundant. But logic is not always the strong point of the legislative process; it remains

---

[53] *Congressional Record*, vol. 80 (1936), p. 3447.
[54] See especially House Report No. 2287, 74th Congress, 2d session (1936), p. 17.

possible (even if unlikely) that the dominant purpose of the act was simply to reaffirm a commitment to the suppression of economically unjustified price discrimination and that the amendments were designed, if ineptly, to further that purpose.

This is not the place for attempting to resolve a difficult issue of statutory interpretation. For our purposes it is sufficient to note that the act and its origins do not enable one to say with confidence whether Congress accepted a view of public policy in this area that would go considerably beyond the suppression of economically unjustifiable price differences, in the interest of fostering small business—or, more accurately, a subset of small businesses in the distribution trades.

Administration of the Act. As had been the case with the original Clayton Act, there were three routes for the redress of violations of section 2 as amended by the Robinson-Patman Act. First, the Department of Justice could bring actions to enjoin such violations. Second, private parties injured by violations of the act could sue for an injunction or for treble damages. Third, the Federal Trade Commission could redress violations through cease-and-desist orders (in effect, injunctions) issued in administrative proceedings. In practice, the burden of enforcement fell on the Federal Trade Commission. In the forty years that the act has been on the books the Department of Justice has brought only a handful of Robinson-Patman actions. Private antitrust suits were in general relatively rare until the late 1940s, and while separate statistics for private actions under the Robinson-Patman Act are not available, it appears that such actions remained rare until quite recently.[55] As part of the enormous upsurge in the number of private actions that began in the early 1960s, the number of private suits under the Robinson-Patman Act has also increased.[56] Even today, however, private Robinson-Patman suits appear to be relatively infrequent. For example, in all of 1975 only nineteen decisions in private Robinson-Patman suits were reported in the federal trial or appellate courts, and eight of these involved other charges under the federal antitrust laws as well as a Robinson-Patman charge.[57] Of course, the reported cases are only a fraction

---

[55] See Richard A. Posner, "A Statistical Study of Antitrust Enforcement," *Journal of Law and Economics*, vol. 13 (1970), pp. 365 and 370-74.

[56] See Posner, *Antitrust Law: An Economic Perspective*, p. 34, Table 4.

[57] Computed from 1975-1 and 1975-2 *Trade Cases*, published by Commerce Clearing House.

of the total—which includes cases that are settled without leaving any trace in the reports—and one does not know in this instance how large a fraction.

Nevertheless, it is clear that the major enforcer of the act has been the Federal Trade Commission. Most, but not all, of the body of official (including judicial) interpretation of the act has been produced either in the decisions of the FTC or by the courts in reviewing FTC orders. Any history of the enforcement of the act must therefore focus on the activities of the Federal Trade Commission.

The history of FTC enforcement can be divided into three stages. In the first, which began with the passage of the act and gradually ended during the 1960s, the thrust of the commission's activity was toward minimizing the scope of the evidentiary inquiry in Robinson-Patman litigation. This was done in two ways. First, enforcement efforts were focused on those provisions of the act (mainly sections 2(c), (d), and (e) of the amended Clayton Act) in which the statute itself appeared to have limited the breadth of the required or permitted inquiry in an adjudicative proceeding: through 1971, of the 1,395 complaints that the commission had brought under the Robinson-Patman Act, 964—almost 70 percent—had been brought under one of these sections.[58] Second, the commission endeavored both to narrow still further the scope of inquiry under these sections and to interpret section 2(a) and the good-faith defense in section 2(b) in such a way as to make section 2(a) a virtually per se prohibition of price differences. In thus attempting a radical streamlining of the statutory provisions, the commission had respectable antecedents in the history of judicial interpretation of section 1 of the Sherman Act, wherein a series of absolute prohibitions (against price fixing, against resale price maintenance, and against certain boycotts and tying arrangements) had been crystallized from rather nebulous statutory language. It was natural that the commission, with its limited resources, should be pushed in the same direction, but it may be doubted that the result of the process was as happy in the regulation of price differences and related marketing practices as it has been in traditional areas of antitrust enforcement.

---

[58] I have not been able to obtain a breakdown of FTC Robinson-Patman complaints by specific offense for the period after 1971. However, only eight such complaints were filed in the 1972 through 1974 fiscal years, according to the FTC's Office of Program Planning, and I believe very few in the last two fiscal years.

The era of mechanical simplification and extension of the Robinson-Patman Act came to an end during (and in part because of) the tenure of Philip Elman as a member of the Federal Trade Commission from 1961 to 1970. In a series of important opinions, Commissioner Elman, sometimes commanding a reluctant majority, sometimes dissenting in an opinion that would point the way for a reviewing court to reverse the commission, chipped away at the per se rules that had been developed in the previous twenty-five years of Robinson-Patman interpretation. This process, described in detail in the next part of this study, was both encouraged and reinforced by an increasing judicial hostility to the commission's Robinson-Patman Act enforcement, and had the result of increasing the scope of the required or permitted factual inquiry in Robinson-Patman cases. The scope of inquiry was increased both in cases brought under the strict sections— 2(c), 2(d), and 2(e)—and in those brought under the basic prohibition of price discrimination in section 2(a). The result was a substantial increase to the commission and its staff in cost and difficulty of trying and winning Robinson-Patman suits. This development led in turn to a marked drop-off in the number of Robinson-Patman complaints filed by the FTC, as shown in Table 1.

In the third and current phase of the commission's enforcement of the Robinson-Patman Act, the disinclination to enforce the act became institutionalized in a policy of seemingly deliberate neglect. This stage can be dated from the appointment of Miles Kirkpatrick as chairman of the commission in 1969. Again as shown in Table 1, at present the level of Robinson-Patman enforcement activity by the commission is very low. It would be erroneous to conclude, however, that the act has been repealed *sub silentio*: a vast body of restrictive doctrine remains memorialized in the precedents of the Federal Trade Commission and of the courts. Although this body of doctrine was liberalized somewhat during the 1960s era, it remains, as we shall see in the next section, anticompetitive. Moreover, the increasing boldness and aggressiveness of the private antitrust bar, coupled with judicial decisions regarding proof of antitrust damages generally, make the Robinson-Patman Act a valued weapon in the armory of private antitrust enforcement; and the private enforcers rely on the body of precedents built up mainly in FTC proceedings and judicial review thereof. Although the course of judicial interpretation in the private actions may in time lead to a further

Table 1

FTC ENFORCEMENT OF THE ROBINSON-PATMAN ACT, 1937–1974

Fiscal Year	Number of Complaints Issued					
	Section 2(a)	Section 2(c)	Section 2(d)	Section 2(e)	Section 2(f)	Total
1937	16	5	5	7	3	36
1938	13	4	1	0	1	19
1939	24	5	3	2	1	35
1940	20	3	12	7	1	43
1941	11	43	2	2	0	58
1942	8	4	4	1	2	19
1943	6	9	0	1	2	18
1944	8	9	4	0	1	22
1945	1	17	3	2	0	23
1946	3	8	0	0	1	12
1947	3	8	1	0	0	12
1948	13	10	10	10	0	43
1949	31	31	28	24	1	115
1950	15	1	1	1	3	22
1951	8	5	4	0	1	18
1952	11	1	2	1	2	17
1953	9	3	1	1	0	14

1954	5	4	4	2	0	15
1955	12	7	1	1	0	21
1956	2	3	21	5	0	31
1957	18	8	16	0	2	44
1958	24	22	20	4	6	76
1959	22	24	24	22	2	74
1960	48	45	43	4	4	144
1961	12	39	49	33	2	105
1962	2	13	26	0	0	41
1963	8	13	192	2	0	215
1964	5	0	20	0	0	25
1965	4	0	7	0	1	12
1966	3	0	10	1	2	16
1967	2	2	3	1	1	9
1968	2	2	0	0	0	4
1969	9	1	1	0	0	11
1970	4	6	0	0	1	11
1971	4	0	5	1	2	12
1972	N.A.	N.A.	N.A.	N.A.	N.A.	1
1973	N.A.	N.A.	N.A.	N.A.	N.A.	1
1974	N.A.	N.A.	N.A.	N.A.	N.A.	6

Source: For 1947-1961, Frederick M. Rowe, *Price Discrimination under the Robinson-Patman Act* (Boston: Little, Brown and Co., 1962), p. 537, Table 11; for 1962-1963, Id., 1964 Supplement, p. 169; for 1964-1971, Commerce Clearing House, *Trade Regulation Reporter*, vol. 3, p. 24,001ff. (FTC Docket of Complaints); for 1972-1974, Federal Trade Commission, Office of Program Planning.

modification of the Robinson-Patman prohibitions, one doubts how fast and how far this process will go since (as was mentioned earlier) there is at least some basis for the view that the Robinson-Patman Act really was intended to go beyond the prevention of economically objectionable price discrimination. One cannot predict either that the course of judicial interpretation alone will purge the act of its undesirable features or that the FTC will remain forever dormant in its enforcement of the act.

III. THE SCOPE AND EFFECT OF THE PRINCIPAL ROBINSON-PATMAN ACT PROHIBITIONS

Price Discrimination. Let us take a closer look now at the language, interpretation, and economic consequences of the Robinson-Patman Act. I shall begin with section 2(a) of the Clayton Act, which—as has been pointed out in the previous part of this study—is a much modified version of section 2 of the original Clayton Act of 1914. The analysis that follows is not intended as a lawyer's guide to compliance with the act; hence it omits much detail that lawyers involved with counseling compliance with the act rightly regard as essential. My purpose is to sketch a general picture of the practical meaning of the act and of the economic consequences of that meaning.

Jurisdictional Limitations. Section 2(a) forbids price discrimination between purchasers of commodities of like grade and quality by a firm selling commodities in interstate commerce where the effect may be to lessen competition substantially, to tend to create a monopoly, or to prevent or destroy competition with any firm.[59]

---

[59] The text of sections 2(a) and 2(b), 15 U.S.C., secs. 13(a), (b), is in pertinent part as follows:

(a) That it shall be unlawful for any person engaged in commerce, in the course of such commerce, either directly or indirectly, to discriminate in price between different purchasers of commodities of like grade and quality, where either or any of the purchases involved in such discrimination are in commerce where such commodities are sold for use, consumption, or resale within the United States or any Territory thereof or any other place under the jurisdiction of the United States, and where the effect of such discrimination may be substantially to lessen competition or tend to create a monopoly in any line of commerce, or to injure, destroy, or prevent competition with any person who either grants or knowingly receives the benefit of such discrimination, or with customers of either of them: *Provided,*

The section contains a number of jurisdictional limitations that greatly reduce the effectiveness of the statute in carrying out whatever purposes might have been in the minds of the enacting congressmen. To begin with, the statute is limited to commodities and thus does not reach services—an artificial and seemingly irrational limitation on its scope. And, unlike other provisions of the Clayton Act, section 2(a) is limited to sales and may therefore be avoided by leasing. Although the significance of these loopholes is reduced by the fact that the Federal Trade Commission can use section 5 of the Federal Trade Commission Act to plug loopholes in the Clayton Act,[60] this solution to the loophole problem is incomplete in that there are no private remedies for violations of section 5 of the Federal Trade Commission Act. It is an open question to what extent section 1 of the Sherman Act might be interpreted as reaching practices that would violate section 2(a) of the Clayton Act if it were not for one of the jurisdictional limitations of section 2(a).

The term *discrimination* in section 2(a) has been interpreted to mean a difference in price. Discriminatory pricing in which the favored and disfavored purchasers are charged the same price is not within the scope of the act. (Again, section 5 of the Federal Trade Commission Act could in principle be used to overcome this limitation.) Furthermore, the price difference must occur in the sale of commodities of like grade and quality: thus a small difference between the goods sold to the favored purchaser and others may serve to avoid the statute. However, one of the basic dilemmas of the statute is that while the "like grade and quality" requirement creates a loophole whereby sell-

---

That nothing herein contained shall prevent differentials which make only due allowance for differences in the cost of manufacture, sale, or delivery resulting from the differing methods or quantities in which such commodities are to such purchasers sold or delivered. . . .

(b) Upon proof being made, at any hearing on a complaint under this section, that there has been discrimination in price or services or facilities furnished, the burden of rebutting the prima facie case thus made by showing justification shall be upon the person charged with a violation of this section, and unless justification shall be affirmatively shown, the Commission is authorized to issue an order terminating the discrimination: *Provided,* a seller rebutting the prima facie case thus made by showing that his lower price or the furnishing of services or facilities to any purchaser or purchasers was made in good faith to meet an equally low price of a competitor, or the services or facilities furnished by a competitor.

[60] See FTC v. Brown Shoe Co., 384 U.S. 316 (1966), and with specific reference to section 2(a) loopholes see also Peelers Co., 65 FTC 699 (1964), enforced *sub nom.* La Peyre v. FTC, 366 F.2d 117 (5th Cir. 1966).

ers may avoid the statute by differentiating their products beyond the point indicated by purely economic considerations, eliminating the requirement might well result in an undue expansion of the prohibitory scope of the statute. This problem is illustrated by the *Borden* case, in which the Supreme Court upheld the FTC's position that physically identical products are of like grade and quality within the meaning of the statute even though one is advertised and sold by the seller under his own trademark (that is, as brand merchandise) and the other is sold without brand identification or seller promotion for resale by the purchaser (normally a chain store) under its own (that is, "private" or "house") brand name.[61] The existence of a price difference in these circumstances cannot, of course, be assumed to reflect price discrimination; generally the reason for the difference is the higher promotional cost incurred by the seller in the sale of his brand merchandise. Yet since, as we are about to see, it is often the case that little more than a price difference is required to establish a violation of section 2(a), the result of deeming the brand and nonbrand sales to be of like grade and quality is to place innocent price differences in serious legal jeopardy.

Section 2(a) is also limited in its terms to a discrimination between *purchasers* from the seller. This limitation has caused the commission endless trouble where the discrimination occurs between firms at different levels in the chain of distribution. For example, a seller might be selling the same product (1) directly to a retailer and (2) to a wholesaler reselling to a retailer who is in competition with the direct-buying retailer. If there is discrimination between the two retailers, it is actionable under the statute only if the retailer purchasing through the wholesaler may somehow be deemed an indirect purchaser from the seller. This has led the commission to the extraordinary anomaly of condoning resale price maintenance (a per se violation of section 1 of the Sherman Act and section 5 of the Federal Trade Commission Act) in cases where the seller's fixing of the wholesaler's price to the retailer enables the commission to deem the retailer an indirect purchaser from the seller.[62] Finally, the act is avoided if the seller sells his entire output to a single purchaser since then he cannot be discriminating between purchasers.

---

[61] FTC v. Borden Co., 383 U.S. 637 (1966).

[62] See, for example, Monroe Auto Equipment Co., 66 FTC 276, 301 (1964) (Commissioner Elman, dissenting), affirmed 347 F.2d 401 (7th Cir. 1965).

In light of the many important jurisdictional limitations in section 2(a), there can be no confidence that its general effect is to benefit some deserving or preferred subset of small businessmen. Doubt on this score is reinforced by the practical limitation of the act's protection to firms engaged in distribution. A manufacturing firm purchases a variety of inputs, of which two of the largest—capital and labor—are outside of the act's coverage, leaving subject to the act only inputs of raw materials, supplies, machinery, and other tangible goods. But it is rare that a single one of these inputs will represent so large a part of the firm's cost of production that a price discrimination favoring a competing purchaser would have sufficient impact on competition to satisfy even the most severely attenuated version of the Robinson-Patman Act's requirement that some competitive injury be proved. It is only in the case of distribution, where on average about a half of the cost of each sale is accounted for by the price of an input that is specific to that sale (namely, the goods that are resold), that price differences have a sufficiently dramatic effect on the cost of particular sales to satisfy the statute's competitive injury requirement.

We are left then with a statute which at most protects only a limited subset of small merchants, consisting of those firms engaged in wholesale or retail distribution of commodities (not services) who purchase from sellers who sell commodities of essentially identical physical characteristics to competing purchasers at different prices. It may be doubted that a group so defined is entitled to describe itself as a segment of the small-business community entitled to special and costly protections against competition. It may also be doubted that a statute so confined to this kind of protection would bear more than an accidental relationship to a policy of preventing or regulating price discrimination as that concept is understood in economic analysis.

Primary-Line Discrimination. Although the primary purpose of the Robinson-Patman amendments to section 2 was to curb secondary-line discrimination (that is, discrimination whose impact is felt in the competition among the buyers from the discriminating seller), the statute is also applicable and has been applied to primary-line discrimination (whose impact is felt by the competitors of the discriminating seller). As pointed out in Section I of this study, it is doubtful that any statute other than the

Sherman Act is needed or appropriate to deal with predatory pricing. In practice, the existence of section 2(a) has served not to plug any gaps in the Sherman Act's coverage of predatory pricing but to forbid (as predatory pricing) price differences that are not inefficient or anticompetitive and that perhaps—although this is not sure—would not be prohibited under the Sherman Act.

The commission over the years has brought many dubious primary-line cases under section 2(a) but the leading case in interpreting section 2(a) as applied to primary-line discrimination, the Supreme Court's *Utah Pie* decision, was a private case.[63] The defendants in that case, several large manufacturers of frozen desserts, sometimes sold their desserts at lower prices in Salt Lake City, where they faced the competition of a local firm that had about two-thirds of the market, than in other parts of the country. Their intent was to take market share away from the local competitor, which was both inevitable and unobjectionable given the dominant position of the local firm—no seller could have increased its share of that market without intending to take sales away from Utah Pie. Although the Court remarked in its opinion that the defendants' prices in Salt Lake City did not cover their full overhead costs, there was no suggestion that these unrecovered overhead costs were marginal costs of selling in Salt Lake City. Accordingly there was no basis for a judgment that the defendants were selling at a price that was inefficiently low. That being so, their prices in other markets were simply irrelevant from the standpoint of preventing predation in Salt Lake City.[64] So far as appears, the price differences on which the decision turned were the result simply of disequilibrium conditions creating temporary non-cost-justified price disparities between Salt Lake City and other markets.

I shall not discuss primary-line price discrimination further in this study. There is no need for a statute that supplements the Sherman Act's prohibitions against predatory pricing; those prohibitions are adequate. The only effect of having an additional statute dealing with primary-line discrimination has been, as in the *Utah Pie* case, to prohibit innocent competitive behavior.

Secondary-Line Discrimination. For secondary-line price discrimination, the most critical issue in the interpretation of section 2(a) is what is to be required in the way of proof of com-

---

[63] Utah Pie Co. v. Continental Baking Co., 386 U.S. 685 (1967).
[64] See pp. 19-20 above.

petitive injury. The polar extremes are (1) to regard a price difference itself as conclusive evidence of anticompetitive effect, on the ground that any firm that pays more than its competitors for goods that it is trying to resell in competition with other firms is at a competitive disadvantage, and (2) to require, as in merger cases brought under the amended section 7 of the Clayton Act, proof that the discrimination is likely to create or contribute to an anticompetitive market structure.[65] The first pole seems untenable in that it reads the competitive-injury requirement right out of the statute. The second may be objected to as giving no weight at all to the "destroy or prevent competition" clause of the competitive-injury standard, a clause that has no counterpart in the other sections of the Clayton Act and was apparently added to section 2(a) in an effort to create a standard of illegality stricter than the normal Clayton Act standard.

In its early cases under section 2(a) the commission pushed hard for an interpretation that would attach a conclusive presumption of anticompetitive effect to any significant discrimination (that is, price difference). This interpretation received strong support from the Supreme Court's opinion in the *Morton Salt* case.[66] However, the facts of that case suggested a somewhat narrower interpretation. At issue were both volume and quantity discounts extended according to established schedules by the Morton Salt Company, and there was some basis for concern that the discriminations, being systematic in character, were likely to have a significant effect on the ability of a disfavored grocery store purchasing from Morton Salt to resell salt in competition with favored purchasers. This distinguishing characteristic of the *Morton Salt* case was invoked many years later in the *American Oil* case by a court of appeals which, following Commissioner Elman's dissent, reversed the commission for holding that it could infer the requisite competitive injury from price differences charged competing retail gasoline dealers during the course of a seventeen-day "price war." [67]

Requiring the commission to prove a persistent and systematic price difference, as in the *American Oil* case, is in principle a method of distinguishing between discrimination that

---

[65] For a muddled but representative and influential statement of the standard under section 7, see Brown Shoe Co. v. United States, 370 U.S. 294 (1962).

[66] FTC v. Morton Salt Co., 334 U.S. 37 (1948).

[67] American Oil Co. v. FTC, 325 F.2d 101 (7th Cir. 1963).

results from the exercise of monopoly power and discrimination that occurs in the process of adjusting to a new equilibrium. Arguably, the first sort of discrimination should be prohibited, while the second should surely be permitted and indeed encouraged. Since the former is systematic and the latter sporadic, an interpretation of the competitive-injury standard of section 2(a) that limited its reach to systematic price discrimination might narrow the act to practices that there is at least some economic basis for condemning. Thus the principle of the *Morton Salt* case as reinterpreted in the *American Oil* case represented an important step toward bringing section 2(a) into line with the economic analysis of price discrimination.

The main problem remaining—if we may assume, perhaps too optimistically, that the *Morton Salt* principle as thus reinterpreted can now be regarded as settled law—is that of confounding price discrimination and cost-justified price differences. Section 2(a) does not require proof that a challenged price difference—a "discrimination" within the meaning of the act—is not justified by a difference in costs. However, it does allow a cost-justification defense. The statutory structure is objectionable: cost justification would be an appropriate matter of defense were there some basis for thinking that most price differences were discriminatory—that is, not cost-justified—but in fact discriminatory prices in the economic sense are surely the exception rather than the rule. A better presumption would be that a price difference *was* cost-justified than that it was not. However, the difference between what is part of the prima facie case and what is part of the defense is unlikely (save possibly in the setting of a jury trial) to be a critical factor in deciding most cases. The main objection to the cost-justification provision in section 2(a) is not that the burden of proof is on the defendant but that the commission has been so niggardly in the scope it has allowed to the cost-justification defense.

This is not the place to examine in detail the contours of the cost-justification defense as they have been fixed by the commission in a long course of interpretation. It is enough to note that the defense has been so interpreted and applied as to make it virtually impossible for firms to justify price differences on the basis of cost differences. Items of genuine economic cost are excluded under arcane and unrealistic cost-accounting principles.[68] As a result many price differences have been held to violate the act although the defendant was prevented from demonstrating the cost basis of the challenged price difference. Thus, the act has in practice undoubtedly operated to suppress price differences that were justified by differences in cost. This is a serious interference with the efficient functioning of the economy. I have already argued that the possible beneficial effects of this interference on the welfare of small business as a whole, or on some appropriately defined subset of small businesses, have been altogether too random to enable such interference to be justified on social grounds.

The inefficiencies caused by section 2(a) enforcement, given the cramped contours of the cost-justification defense, are illustrated by a series of cases in which the commission attacked discounts granted automobile parts jobbers who do their own warehousing.[69] The jobbers had demanded and received the right to purchase from parts manufacturers at the warehouse-distributor price rather than at the jobber price—this jobber price being the price paid by competing jobbers buying from independent warehouse distributors.[70] The "discrimination" was systematic yet not suggestive of price discrimination in the economic sense of the term. The fact that the jobbers were doing their own warehouse distribution relieved the manufacturer of having to perform the warehousing function for those distributors himself or of having to "buy" warehouse distribution from an independent distributor by selling to him at the warehouse-distributor price. But although the lower price to the warehousing jobbers appears to have reflected a genuine cost difference between them and jobbers who did no warehousing, the cost-justification defense was unusable. The cost savings to the manufacturer could not be demonstrated with the precision required

---

[68] For a good summary of the problems with the defense see Phillip Areeda, *Antitrust Analysis: Problems, Text, Cases,* 2d ed. (Boston: Little, Brown and Co., 1974), pp. 885-88.

[69] For example, Mueller Co. v. FTC, 323 F.2d 44 (7th Cir. 1964); Monroe, note 61 above; Purolator Prods., Inc. v. FTC, 352 F.2d 874 (7th Cir. 1965); National Parts Warehouse, 63 FTC 1692 (1963).

[70] These are the cases in which, as mentioned earlier, the commission used the fact that the manufacturer had fixed the price at which the independent warehouse distributors resold to jobbers as the basis for holding that the jobbers were "indirect purchasers" from the manufacturer and hence that the difference between the jobber price and the warehouse-distributor price at which jobbers who did their own warehousing were permitted to buy was a discrimination between purchasers within the meaning of section 2(a).

by the commission since the manufacturer made no direct sales to non-warehousing jobbers. Only if the manufacturer had done some warehousing himself could he have shown the savings to him from being able, in effect, to contract out the warehousing function to the jobbers and compensate them for performing it by granting them a price lower than the jobber price.

The result of the auto-parts cases has been to frustrate the efforts of buyers to economize on their input costs by combining successive distribution functions in one enterprise. And these decisions cannot possibly be justified as promoting the interests of small business. The FTC's principal target in this area has been cooperative buying groups consisting of small jobbers,[71] and the principal beneficiaries of the commission's enforcement efforts have been the independent warehouse distributors, a group of firms generally larger than the jobbers.

The remaining section 2(a) issue that I shall discuss here is the good-faith meeting of competition defense, set forth in section 2(b). In the early period of enforcement, the commission hedged about the section 2(b) defense with so many limitations that it became practically unusable. But the defense was greatly liberalized in the 1960s. In the important *Callaway* case, for example, the Court of Appeals for the Fifth Circuit, again following the direction charted for it in a dissenting opinion by Commissioner Elman, held that the defense was not unavailable merely because the seller had used a systematic schedule of discounts rather than attempting to meet competitors' price reductions on a spot basis.[72] This meant that a seller could respond to a volume or quantity discount schedule such as had been involved in the *Morton Salt* case by publishing a comparable schedule of his own.

The commission's effort to read section 2(b) out of the statute, while it cannot be condoned, can readily be understood, for if it were interpreted liberally the section 2(b) defense could destroy section 2(a). If every seller in a market could defend his discriminatory pricing practices by reference to comparable discriminations on the part of its competitors, how could the circle be broken and a marketwide practice of discrimination eliminated? Commissioner Elman, in his dissenting opinion in the *Callaway*

---

[71] See, for example, Alhambra Motor Parts, 68 FTC 1039 (1965).

[72] Callaway Mills Co. v. FTC, 362 F.2d 435 (5th Cir. 1966). See also Foster Mfg. Co. v. FTC, 335 F.2d 47 (1st Cir. 1964); but compare Surprise Brassiere Co. v. FTC, 406 F.2d 711 (5th Cir. 1969).

case, was aware of the difficulty and suggested that the commission use its rule-making powers to deal with the problem on a marketwide basis. An appealing solution in principle, this raises numerous practical problems that the commission has not been able to resolve. Another possibility would be to require the seller to prove that the price he is meeting is a lawful one. But this is an unreasonable constriction of the defense, not only because the seller is in no position to develop such proof but also because the illegality of the price he is meeting does not lessen the urgency for him to meet the price in order to remain in the market.

The section 2(b) defense has a fundamental logic behind it despite the difficulties that it creates for enforcement. If discrimination is widespread in any market, a proceeding to forbid discriminatory pricing by only one or a handful of the sellers in that market cannot have a significant economic (or other) impact. Purchasers who were previously receiving discriminatorily low prices from firms that will now be forbidden to grant such discounts will simply switch their patronage to firms against which the commission has not yet proceeded, and the competitive impact of the discounts on competitors of the favored purchasers will be the same.

To recapitulate, the courts in recent years, by distinguishing between systematic and merely sporadic price differences and placing on the commission (or other Robinson-Patman plaintiff) a substantial burden of proving competitive injury when only a sporadic discrimination is alleged, have to some degree confined section 2(a) to price differences involving the type of price discrimination that is objectionable on economic grounds. However, most price differences—even of the systematic sort—are not the result of price discrimination but merely reflect differences in cost. As a result of the narrow interpretation that has been placed on the cost-justification defense, many cost-justified price differences have been suppressed in the name of preventing discrimination. Meanwhile, the recent liberalization of the good-faith meeting-of-competition defense contained in section 2(b) of the act has undermined the entire statute by making it extremely difficult for the commission to proceed effectively against discrimination that is marketwide—but where discrimination is marketwide, proceeding against a minority of the sellers is unlikely to have any significant impact on competitive relations. To the extent that the meeting-competition defense is taken seriously and applied fairly, the act is unlikely to have much impact on price differences. However, it should be noted that even if there were no such defense, and even if the statute did not have the loopholes discussed above, it is unlikely that the commission, by proceeding piecemeal against a few sellers in markets in which discrimination or price differences were rampant, would have more than a slight impact on competitive relations.

In short, the price discrimination offense, as defined in the statute and interpreted by the courts and the commission, would have pernicious effects were it effective in stamping out all of the price differences (many cost-based or merely transitory) that are arguably unlawful under the act. But it has probably not been effective.

Section 2(c). Section 2(c) of the Clayton Act, a provision added to the statute by the Robinson-Patman amendments, forbids the payment of brokerage—or of a discount or allowance in lieu of brokerage—to an agent of the opposite party to the transaction, except for services rendered.[73] The statute was aimed at the practice whereby large retail food chains such as A&P demanded and received compensation from their suppliers for purchasing without the intermediation of a food broker, traditionally a seller's agent who assembles the output of a number of small producers for shipment to the food distributor. Congress believed, or professed to believe, that A&P and the other chains were demanding spurious brokerage payments from the sellers as a disguised form of price discrimination, without rendering any of the services that a broker would render. The main purpose of the statute, ostensibly at least, was, by forbidding phony brokerage, to force all price discriminations into the open where they could be dealt with under section 2(a).[74]

---

[73] The text of section 2(c), 15 U.S.C., sec. 13(c), is as follows:

> (c) That it shall be unlawful for any person engaged in commerce, in the course of such commerce, to pay or grant, or to receive or accept, anything of value as a commission, brokerage, or other compensation, or any allowance or discount in lieu thereof, except for services rendered in connection with the sale or purchase of goods, wares, or merchandise, either to the other party to such transaction or to an agent, representative, or other intermediary therein where such intermediary is acting in fact for or in behalf, or is subject to the direct or indirect control, of any party to such transaction other than the person by whom such compensation is so granted or paid.

[74] See House Report No. 2287, 74th Congress, 2d session (1936), pp. 14-15.

Had section 2(c) been so interpreted from the start, there would have been little serious objection to it. But instead of interpreting it this way the FTC took the position that payment of brokerage—or of an allowance in lieu of brokerage—to the agent of the other party to the transaction was unlawful regardless of the services rendered by the buyer. In principle, at least, a seller could never compensate the buyer for adopting a method of purchase that enabled his dispensing with the services of a food broker, because that would mean paying brokerage or an allowance in lieu of brokerage to the other party to the transaction or his agent. The "except for services rendered" clause in the statute was ignored.

So interpreted, the statute became a charter protecting food brokers from the competition of alternative forms of distribution. Moreover, the streamlined contours of the section 2(c) offense as defined by the commission invited the heavy concentration of enforcement resources in this unworthy area shown in Table 1. But, once again, in the 1960s the commission was induced (with judicial assistance) to resuscitate the "except for services rendered" provision in section 2(c) and to confine the statutory prohibition to brokerage payments or allowances that were in fact forms of price discrimination rather than compensation for services rendered, albeit not by a seller's broker.[75]

Yet there is still a great deal of confusion about the meaning of section 2(c). This is due in part to the opinion of the Supreme Court in the *Broch* case.[76] In that case a buyer demanded a discount and the seller refused to grant the discount if he had to pay the full brokerage commission to his broker. The seller went to the broker and asked him to accept a reduction in his normal brokerage commission so that the deal could be made. The broker agreed and was then sued by the commission for having been a party to an illegal brokerage transaction. The commission's theory, which the Supreme Court adopted, was that the discount to the buyer was in lieu of brokerage since it was made possible by the broker's agreeing to accept a reduction in his normal brokerage commission. This application of section 2(c) is, however, totally perverse once it is accepted that the purpose of that statute is to force price discriminations disguised as brokerage payments into the open. There was no element of concealment in the *Broch* case.

---

[75] See, for example, Tillie Lewis Foods, Inc., 65 FTC 1099 (1964); Thomasville Chair Co. v. FTC, 306 F.2d 541 (5th Cir. 1962).

[76] FTC v. Henry Broch & Co., 363 U.S. 166 (1960).

The seller was granting the buyer an *explicit* price discount and if it was discriminatory the price discrimination was out in the open for everyone to see. The broker was involved only in having enabled the explicit discount to be granted by accepting a reduction in his normal broker's commission. No discount or payment denominated as brokerage or as an allowance in lieu of brokerage was given to the buyer.

The Supreme Court rejected the idea that the only purpose of section 2(c) was to eliminate phony brokerage, though also in its opinion, and inconsistently, it rejected the idea that section 2(c) is designed to prevent discounts made possible by changes in traditional brokerage methods and compensation. The *Broch* case is thus something of an obstacle to confining section 2(c) to phony brokerage, thereby making it inapplicable whenever there is either an explicit discount or a discount which—although denominated as being for brokerage or in lieu of brokerage—is justifiable because services were actually rendered to the seller by the buyer or buyer's agent in the transaction.

The greatest irony of section 2(c) is that it has so often been used to oppress small business. Many of the defendants in section 2(c) cases have been buying cooperatives composed of small food stores, which sought to obtain a discount for having adopted methods of centralized purchasing that dispensed with a need for a food broker and so made them more competitive with the chain stores.[77] And the principal beneficiaries of section 2(c) have been food brokers, seemingly not a specially deserving group of small businessmen—or even a group of particularly small businessmen.

Section 2(d). The last provision of the Robinson-Patman Act that I shall discuss in this study is section 2(d), which forbids the furnishing of advertising allowances (normally made for point-of-sale advertising of goods manufactured by the seller and sold at retail by the buyer) unless the allowances are made available on proportionately equal terms to all competing purchasers.[78] As

---

[77] See Rowe, *Price Discrimination under the Robinson-Patman Act*, pp. 539-40.

[78] The text of section 2(d), 15 U.S.C., sec. 13(d), is as follows:

(d) That it shall be unlawful for any person engaged in commerce to pay or contract for the payment of anything of value to or for the benefit of a customer of such person in the course of such commerce as compensation or in consideration for any services or facilities furnished by or through such customer in connection with the processing, handling, sale or offering for sale of any products or

with the brokerage clause, the ostensible purpose of this provision was to force price discriminations disguised as advertising allowances into the open where they could be dealt with under section 2(a).[79] Rather than forbidding spurious or fraudulent advertising allowances, however, Congress required that advertising allowances be proportioned among competing purchasers. Such a provision invites use as a device for subsidizing retail merchants who carry so small a volume of any seller's goods that but for the act no seller would provide them with a point-of-sale advertising allowance—the administrative expense would exceed the advertising value to the seller. And for many years the commission was loath to permit sellers to establish a cutoff point below which the volume of goods carried by the retail merchant was simply too small for it to be economical to provide him with an advertising allowance. In recent years, as part of the general liberalizing trend in the interpretation of the act, reasonable cutoff points have been allowed, but the statute continues to impede sellers in allocating point-of-sale advertising allowances in a way that would maximize the value to them of point-of-sale advertising. The requirement of proportional equality, as interpreted, does not adequately recognize the differences in advertising value among different types of retail outlet, or the costs of giving small allowances to small outlets when that is the price of being permitted to grant large allowances to large outlets.

In a way, section 2(d)—and its companion provision 2(e)—is even more anomalous than section 2(c). If limited to phony brokerage, section 2(c) is perhaps defensible as a means of preventing the concealment of price discrimination under the guise of brokerage and the consequent evasion of section 2(a). Section 2(d), however, lacking as it does any counterpart to the "except for services rendered" proviso of 2(c), cannot be so limited. It requires even genuine advertising allowances to be granted on terms of proportional equality to all competing retailers—and this no matter whether the lack of proportionality causes competitive injury, and regardless of the economic justifi-

---

commodities manufactured, sold, or offered for sale by such person, unless such payment or consideration is available on proportionally equal terms to all other customers competing in the distribution of such products or commodities.

A related section, 2(e), which I shall not discuss separately, governs the provision of the advertising materials, et cetera, themselves as distinct from a money allowance for advertising.

[79] See House Report No. 2287.

cations for lack of proportionality (save as such justifications may perhaps be implicit in the very concept of proportionality). The short of it is that the Robinson-Patman Act subjects advertising allowances, even where wholly genuine, to a stricter scrutiny than explicit price discounts—and there is no conceivable justification for this.

Special problems in the application of section 2(d) are created when (as is not uncommon) a seller sells both directly to some retailers and indirectly through wholesalers to other retailers who compete with the direct-buying retailers. The Supreme Court has held that if such a seller grants advertising allowances to the direct-buying retailers, it must grant comparable allowances to its wholesalers and somehow see that the allowances are passed on to the retailers who purchase from the wholesalers.[80] The result is an administrative nightmare for the seller. Also, a seller's efforts to require his purchasers to pass on an allowance to someone further down the chain of distribution may result in his violating section 1 of the Sherman Act, which has been interpreted as strictly limiting the imposition of restrictions on the resale of goods.[81]

The last point illustrates a general problem with the Robinson-Patman Act—its inconsistency with the Sherman Act. I am not so much concerned here with the inconsistency between the FTC's efforts to encourage seller control of middlemen and the Sherman Act's strictures against the impositions of restrictions on distribution, which I think are excessive.[82] Rather, I am concerned with the effect of the Robinson-Patman Act in encouraging cartel pricing. I noted earlier that discriminatory price reductions are a common method by which price-fixing agreements are eroded. Even with recent judicial efforts to limit the prohibitions of the act to systematic (rather than sporadic) discrimination, the act as currently interpreted inhibits competitive price reductions. It has been held, for example, that exchanges of price information among competitors that would otherwise violate the Sherman Act because of their dampening effect on price competition are permissible where necessary to protect a seller from inadvertently granting an unlawful discount to a buyer who has misrepresented the price at which he could purchase from a competitor of the

[80] See FTC v. Fred Meyer, Inc., 390 U.S. 341 (1968).

[81] See, for example, United States v. Arnold Schwinn & Co., 388 U.S. 365 (1967).

[82] See Posner, *Antitrust Law: An Economic Perspective*, pp. 165-66.

seller.[83] In the *Kroger* case a buyer was actually held to have violated section 2(f) of the Clayton Act [84] because he had misrepresented a discount available from another seller and thereby knowingly induced his seller to grant him a discriminatory price reduction.[85] Such a decision, by removing a source of uncertainty among sellers concerning their competitors' actions, increases the cohesion of price-fixing conspiracies.

This completes a necessarily rather cursory survey of a statute which, in decades of often contradictory interpretations, has produced an enormous body of legal doctrine, giving employment to many lawyers. As I emphasized at the outset, I have not tried to write a lawyer's guide to the interpretation and application of the Robinson-Patman Act, but rather to summarize the major features of the act in the course of subjecting it to an economic and social evaluation. The conclusion of such an evaluation must be negative. While, as I pointed out in Section I, there is an economic case for the regulation of price discrimination, the Robinson-Patman Act cannot be considered a remotely suitable method for achieving such a goal. Section 2(a) is the central provision, yet its utility as an instrument for the prevention of harmful forms of price discrimination is doubtful in the extreme, and certainly it discourages a variety of socially desirable price differences. Section 2(c) would appear to be nothing more than a bit of special-interest legislation, and sections 2(d) and 2(e) are impediments to efficient allocation of advertising resources. Nor can the act be defended as an appropriate method of subsidizing deserving small businessmen. It remains to consider only whether the act could be amended in ways that might align it more closely with a proper economic or social concern with discriminatory or differential pricing.

IV. REFORMING THE ROBINSON-PATMAN ACT

Could the Robinson-Patman Act be salvaged by amendment or should it be discarded? I incline to the latter view.

Over the years there have been many proposals for amending the Robinson-Patman Act. It would extend this study unduly to

---

[83] See Belliston v. Texaco, Inc., 455 F.2d 175 (10th Cir. 1972); Wall Products Co. v. National Gypsum Co., 326 F. Supp. 295 (N.D. Calif. 1971).

[84] See p. 27 above.

[85] Kroger, Inc. v. FTC, 438 F.2d 1372 (6th Cir. 1969).

discuss all of them. The most careful and thoughtful of the proposals is that of the White House Task Force on Antitrust Policy (Neal Task Force),[86] and that will be the focus of my discussion. As we shall see, the task force's proposal bristles with difficulties that suggest the impracticability of amending the act. Since any significantly anticompetitive practice is certain to violate section 1 or 2 of the Sherman Act, the repeal of the Robinson-Patman Act would not leave any gap in the control of genuinely anticompetitive practices. To be sure, there are many errant interpretations of the Sherman Act: that fact is an argument for the procedure followed by the Neal Task Force—drafting a carefully limited price-discrimination law and then providing expressly that any practice permissible under that law cannot be attacked under the Sherman Act. However, an examination of the specific wording changes proposed by the Neal Task Force suggests that we would be better off with the Sherman Act's prohibitions, notwithstanding the discretion they inevitably give the judiciary to suppress as monopolistic practices that are not truly so.

The amendments proposed by the Neal Task Force include an attempt to define primary-line price discrimination. A glance at the proposed statutory language [87] will reveal the interpretive problems created by any attempt to cast in statutory language a properly limited rule against predatory pricing. The amendment

---

[86] The report of the task force may be found in *Small Business and the Robinson-Patman Act*, Hearings before the Special Subcommittee on Small Business and the Robinson-Patman Act of the House Select Committee on Small Business, 91st Congress, 1st session (1969), vol. 1, pp. 291, 303-5, 317-23, in *Journal of Reprints for Antitrust Law and Economics*, vol. 1 (1969), p. 633, and elsewhere. It is discussed in detail in Erwin A. Elias, "Robinson-Patman: Time for Rechiseling," *Mercer Law Review*, vol. 26 (1975), p. 689ff.

[87] *Small Business and the Robinson-Patman Act*, p. 318:

> The person granting the discrimination is in competition with others serving significantly more limited areas (territories or classes of customers which are relevant lines of commerce), the discrimination is restricted to one or more such limited areas (representing a small part of the total area served by the person granting the discrimination), the consideration exacted in such limited areas is less than the reasonably anticipated long-run average cost of serving those areas (including capital costs), and the discrimination imminently threatens to eliminate from such a limited area one or more competitors whose survival is significant to maintenance of competition in that area.
>
> *Provided, however*, that the survival of a competitor is not significant to the maintenance of competition where, in the line of commerce or area affected, the number of competitors remaining, or the ease with which new competitors may enter, indicates that effective competition will not be suppressed for an appreciable period of time.

would introduce into the law such novel concepts as "serving significantly more limited areas," "a small part of the total area served by the person granting the discrimination," "reasonably anticipated long-run average cost . . . including capital cost," "imminently threatens," and "competitors whose survival is significant to the maintenance of competition"—and each of these necessarily imprecise phrases could be expected to generate a wilderness of precedents. If I had to propose an alternative statutory formulation, I would favor a much simpler one that would codify what I understand to be the existing Sherman Act prohibition of predatory pricing. But I would much prefer relying on interpretation of the Sherman Act to trying to freeze the concept of predatory pricing in statutory language that will inevitably come to have a life of its own.

On the question of secondary-line discrimination, the task force tried to codify the rule of the *Morton Salt* case. But in attempting to distinguish systematic from sporadic discrimination, it again used language that provides an invitation to endless controversy. The key phrase in the amended provision is the requirement of proving that the discrimination was "part of a pattern which systematically favors larger competitors over their smaller rivals." [88] It is unclear whether the intention is to limit the statute to discriminations in favor of large firms and against small or whether the plaintiff need show only that the discrimination was keyed to the volume or quantity of the favored buyer's purchases and hence likely to favor the relatively large purchaser (which might be a small firm) from the discriminating seller. (A discrimination might systematically favor smaller firms in a market where they are the larger purchasers from the particular discriminating seller.) This ambiguity could no doubt be eliminated by appropriate rewording, but even that would still leave problems of proving "pattern" and "system"—problems that, although they are implicit in any price-discrimination case brought under the Sherman Act, seem bound to create greater confusion when frozen in statutory language. In my opinion it would be much better to rely on the concept of a substantial anticompetitive practice implicit in section 1 of the Sherman Act.

The task force recommended a modest broadening of the cost-justification defense and a further liberalization of the section 2(b) meeting-competition defense. It recognized that the meeting-competition defense might give every seller in an indus-

---

[88] Ibid.

try immunity although all were engaged in discrimination, but suggested that in such a case the Federal Trade Commission seek injunctive relief against all of the sellers. However, the practical difficulties of obtaining industry-wide injunctive relief were not discussed, and the practicality of the statute may consequently be doubted. Finally, among other changes, the task force recommended that a test of competitive injury be added to sections 2(c), 2(d), and 2(e), thus bringing them into line with section 2(a).

I suspect that the effect (and perhaps the covert intention) of the Neal Task Force's proposals for amendment of the Robinson-Patman Act would be the strangulation of the act by the interpretive complexities that the amendments would create, or its paralysis by the liberalized good-faith meeting-competition defense that it proposed. The task force's approach may represent a defensible strategy of effective repeal from a political standpoint but that is not a matter which I am competent to judge. Considering the issue without regard to political feasibility, I am persuaded that amending the act is not the proper path to follow. Any statutory revision of the Robinson-Patman Act would require a complex drafting effort, the result of which—after the inevitable errors and compromises of the legislative drafting process—would be a statute that, like the original Robinson-Patman Act, would come to have a life of its own. It would be badly integrated with the other antitrust statutes. It would either forbid too much and thus repeat the unhappy experience of the existing act, or it would forbid too little in which event either it would be ignored (if Sherman Act price-discrimination suits were not preempted as the Neal Task Force recommended) or we would simply have exchanged the vice of over-inclusion for the vice of under-inclusion.

Now it may well be that, despite the various economic objections to price discrimination covered in Section I of this study, there are not enough serious instances either of predatory pricing or of secondary-line price discrimination to warrant the considerable costs of attempting to regulate or prohibit either practice. In that event an approach like that of the Neal Task Force, to narrow the existing act and then make the jurisdiction of the revised act exclusive, may be the wisest after all.

My own preference, however, is for a repeal of the act. Repeal would allow the problem of price discrimination to be approached in the incremental and evolutionary fashion of judicial interpretation of the Sherman Act. It may seem quixotic to advocate the repeal of so firmly established a part of our public policy as the Robinson-Patman Act. But in these days of legislative ferment, which have recently seen the repeal of a seemingly as well established part of our competitive policy—the "fair trade" exemption in the Sherman and Federal Trade Commission acts—it would be reckless to dismiss out of hand the prospects even for so far-reaching a statutory reform as the repeal of Robinson-Patman.

ACT-8801   4/12/95

KF
1627
P68
1976a